THE
EXPERIMENT:

America's
Insanity by
Design

I0137257

Francis William Nicholson II

F W N II Publishing

F W N II Publishing

ISBN: 978-0-578-16291-1

PRINTED IN THE UNITED STATES OF AMERICA

Contents

Acknowledgments

To my dear family, who never fully understood what was happening to me.

To my mother for her unwavering love, to my father for his love and financial support, and to my sister for her love, protection, and legal support.

Preface

Do you know what it is like to never be alone? Have you ever experienced extreme paranoia? Have you ever endured clinical depression? Have you ever explored the good and bad sides of mania? Have you ever feared for your life?

Were any of these experiences real? Was it reality or a defect of the mind? Insanity or at least temporary insanity? Not as defined by the courts but as defined by one's ability to control one's own mind.

I am familiar with these problems of the mind. My brain has experienced all of the above questions. But what set these psychological problems into motion? What caused my brain to function in these fashions? My parents and I have spent a lot of time and money investigating these questions.

The purpose of this book is not to discredit the profession of psychiatry or raise any fears about our government. Rather, it is to explain my interpretation of reality. Psychiatrists have diagnosed me as both paranoid delusional and bipolar schizoaffective. No one accepts my conclusion. Everyone is sympathetic to my explanation, but no one admits knowledge or submits proof of my situation.

Are you ready for a twist? You probably thought this book was going to be about the plight of a mentally ill person. It is, but my explanation is quite a bit different from the average recovering patient. That is a patient that everyone believes to be of sound mind. You be the judge: am I sane or insane? Is my interpretation of reality real or delusional?

This book is based on a series of delusions that I experienced prior to coming to my final conclusion. It was not until I found myself holed up in a hotel room in St. Andrews, Scotland, in 1994 that I realized the truth! Prior to that time, I believed that I suffered from a mental disorder caused by stress and heredity. Now, twenty years later, I know the truth, but I am not better off than before. I cannot do anything to stop the voice in my head.

My conclusion: I am subject to biological and psychological experiments by the US federal government. Sounds like I'm not cured yet, doesn't it? Fifteen psychiatrists and five psychologists have tried to convince me otherwise, but I always return to the same conclusion. I firmly believe the Experiment is going on right now and has been for the majority of my life.

I know. I'm crazy. Or am I right on the money? I invite you to read this book. If you think I'm crazy, it will give you an in-depth look into the insanity of the mind. If you believe my conclusion, this book will provide you, I hope, with a possible explanation of good research for betterment of science, as well as a description of the horror and negligence of unconstitutional action taken by our government.

Foreword

I had a fairly normal upbringing. My father was in the meat-packing business. He started out as a cattle buyer and worked his way up to become president of both Exel and Val-Agra. This meant that as a small child, my family moved around a lot.

I was born in Hawarden, Iowa. Then my family moved to Sioux City, Iowa. Later, my father took a plant manager position in Rockport, Missouri. While my father was plant manager, my family lived in Watson, Missouri, about twenty miles away from Rockport. Next, we moved to Plainview, Texas, where my father took a group vice president position. During the time we lived in Plainview, my mother commuted between Plainview and Lubbock, Texas. She earned a master's degree in interior design at Texas Tech in Lubbock. Finally, we moved to Wichita, Kansas, where I remained until I graduated from high school.

My family arrived in Wichita in 1976, which was the beginning of third grade for me. Initially, I attended a Catholic grade school, but I did not like it. So my mother and father enrolled me into a public grade school, Minaha. Upon graduation from the sixth grade, I went to Blessed Sacrament for junior high, which was another Catholic school. During high school, I attended two private schools, the first being Catholic.

The first high school that I attended was Kapaun Mount Karmel, a popular Catholic high school. During the beginning of my sophomore year, I was expelled for calling a substitute teacher in French class a bitch. My parents then decided, after a heated debate with both the faculty and me, that I should attend Wichita Collegiate School. This was probably the best move of my academic career. The quality education I received at WCS was superior even to my later college education.

I was one of the lucky ones. I had the privilege of growing up in a stable and somewhat affluent household. It was also a household full of love. My mother and father are still married today. My parents always supported me and encouraged me to succeed. They also encouraged me to take part in a multitude of extracurricular activities. My activities included the following: photography, sailboat racing, golf, and airplane flying. I started flying airplanes at the age of sixteen and earned my private pilot's license on my seventeenth birthday.

When it came time to go to college, I attended Arizona State. There was, however, some pressure from my parents to attend a better school. My sister was attending Dartmouth at that time. Therefore, in the spring of my freshman year, I applied to a number of colleges. I decided to attend the University of Wisconsin–Madison. I was accepted to UW Madison at the last minute, during the summer of my freshman year. This may have been when the experimentation began—more on that in a moment.

At the University of Wisconsin, I discovered recreational drugs: marijuana, hallucinogenic mushrooms, and cocaine. This took a large toll on my academic success. After I was placed on academic probation for the second time after four semesters at UW Madison, my father decided that it would be in my best interest to change schools again. He offered to pay the remainder of my college education at one of two institutions, the University of Nebraska–Lincoln or Kansas State, in Manhattan. I chose Nebraska, where I earned a Bachelor of Arts degree in economics.

I do not know for sure when the experimentation began. Wisconsin makes sense. While I attended this institution, I experienced a lot of déjà vu. Thinking back to this time, I remember certain subtle events that took place, which are similar to things I have experienced as a direct result of the Experiment. However, I can guarantee with certainty that the Experiment was in full swing by January of 1993.

Besides the regular head games the operators of the Experiment play with me on a daily basis, there are four basic things that they can control. The first is an internal voice, which is piped in through my head. This internal voice plagues me each and every day, all day long. The second is an external voice—the operators of the Experiment can use my own speech to say whatever they want. The doctors call this an oral hallucination. The third is very common for bipolar people: hearing voices at a distance. An example of this is hearing voices in the rafters or from inside walls. I have experienced this on very few occasions. The final and scariest thing the operators of the Experiment can do is total body control. This includes muscle movement, control of the nervous system, control of bodily functions, and control over both the firing of neurons and the chemical balances of the brain.

Introduction: Take My Word for It

When did I know? After returning from the United Kingdom in 1994, I totally understood what was happening to me. That was when I realized what the operators of the Experiment were capable of doing to me. However, I still have not found out how the control over me is achieved.

But what about the subconscious? Could my subconscious mind distinguish what came from me and what came from the operators of the Experiment? The ego and the id are tricky and deceptive. Was my subconscious picking up on the operators of the Experiment as early as 1988? The operators have the ability to interfere with my dreams as well as playing canned dreams they have created. This is much like going to a movie, except I am asleep. When did the operators begin this practice? Throughout my time on the exchange floor, strange things took place that I will point out as the book progresses. Did these strange happenings inform the sub-consciousness and not the consciousness?

When I moved to Aspen, these happenings became more frequent and bewildering. Later you will learn that the lovely people at Charter Lakeside Hospital convinced me that I was paranoid delusional before my discharge, and Dr. Underhill sealed the door with bipolar. Every doctor had me believing I was insane. This was initially accepted by the conscious mind and made me mistrust my own thoughts and ignore strange occurrences. Basically, I believed I was either bipolar or paranoid delusional.

The problem of dividing out the tricks by the operators from my own actions is extremely difficult. However, hindsight is twenty-twenty. I will discuss the voice prior to the infamous night at the inn in St. Andrews, Scotland. The subconscious mind probably knew, but the conscious mind was very confused prior to this experience.

Three things to remember: I have an internal voice, which gives a constant running commentary throughout the day. This is called a hallucination by the shrinks. I also have an external voice, or spoken voice controlled by the operators. This is called an oral hallucination by the shrinks. The last thing is the operators have total muscular movement control over my body. The shrinks do NOT have a name for this; in fact, they say it is a psychological fallacy belief (I guess that's a name).

Body control coupled with the external voice is the hardest to deal with. When I am left alone and along for the ride, it's definitely a freakish experience. And when they give me back control, I have to clean up the mess!

Also, the names in this manuscript have been changed to protect my friends and free myself and my publisher from liability.

CHAPTER 1

In the Beginning

After graduating from Nebraska, I returned home to Wichita. This enabled me to go back to working at Brick's clothing store. I had worked at Brick's throughout my college summers and Christmas breaks. Brick's was an upper echelon retailer featuring such brands as Hicky Friedman, Burberry, Axis, Zegna, Zennella, Giorgio Armani, and Hugo Boss.

At that time, fall of 1990, my father was working as a commodities trader in Memphis, Tennessee, with the firm Beathan Trading. He was commuting on the weekends to Wichita. My mother chose to remain in Wichita until our house sold. Meanwhile, she was one of Wichita's premier interior designers.

Guess what? Brick's was a poor choice of employment in my father's eyes, even though working the fall season was the best time for commissions. This job would have yielded me at least forty thousand dollars annually, if I had remained.

Every weekend my father would return home and bitch about

me working at Brick's. He would ask, "Do you want to be a clothing salesman the rest of your life?" I would counter, "I think Brick's is a good place to work, with steady income, and I have a good chance of meeting some of Wichita's most influential people." My father's rebuttal would include backing me into a corner and lecturing me with his blood-red face and his finger of authority pointed at my nose. "Billy, you're behind; you took too long [five years] to graduate college. You need to find a real job for your future."

So I suggested a career in aviation to my father; what a mistake that was. At the top of his lungs, he shouted, "Do you want to be a glorified bus driver the rest of your life? No, you cannot be a pilot." So I continued to work at Brick's until something else came along.

Then, much to my surprise my father flew home in a jovial mood the following weekend. The next day, he asked me, "Do you want some help in finding a career?" "What kind of a job?" I inquired. "A job on the COMEX floor in New York." Finally, something we could agree on. I was ecstatic. I had always had an interest in a trading position.

The next week I was to fly to New York City to interview with John Webster's firm, the Tudor Group, Bell Weather.

CHAPTER **2**

The Tudor Group

I flew into New York City for an interview with the Tudor Group, Bell Weather, John Webster's mega million-dollar commodities enterprise. This interview was arranged by James Crown, a wealthy Southern gentleman who raised money for Beathan Trading and my father. James was one of the quality people who worked at Beathan Trading.

Benjamin Oxby, a childhood friend and old boyfriend of my sister, arranged for me to stay at the Leash Club on Sixty-Third Street between Madison Avenue and Park Avenue in Manhattan.

I woke up in the morning at the Leash Club, took a shower, put on my best Armani suit, and got ready for my interview. I was definitely overdressed.

Just prior to leaving the Leash Club for my interview, I received a phone call from my father. My father told me on the phone, "Billy, you cannot work for John Webster." I asked why. He replied, "Because Max Beathan hates John Webster, and it is a conflict of interest for me." I replied, "Then what the fuck am I doing in New York? Didn't James arrange this interview?" To this, my father countered, "Just enjoy the interview, and if they offer you a job, tell them you will need to discuss it with your father." "What a bunch of crap," I responded. Then my father said, "Don't look at that way—consider it a warm-up interview. Max has a plan for you in Chicago."

Already Max Beathan was a strong derailer in my life. Needless to say, I did not try very hard in the interview. I was first given a tour of Bell Weather's office and then the COMEX trading floor. When I went back upstairs to the office, I hung out with the traders for a brief while. They warned me about the personnel lady and said, if I could get by her, I would probably land a job.

My interview with Grace did not go very well. She was a bit of a bitch. (I am sure John wanted a tough operator, and she was.) I did not turn on the charm and promoted Beathan Trading and Exel instead. I did not receive a job offer.

Thinking back, this would have been a golden opportunity for me to work for the Tudor Group, Bell Weather. This trading organization was top-notch, and John's firm did nothing but roll out the red carpet for me!

I flew back to Wichita somewhat dumbfounded.

The possibility does exist that this was planned out, among James, Max, my father, and John Webster, and I was never supposed to get job from the get-go. I'll never know.

CHAPTER 3

The Smear

After spending a short time in Wichita, I flew to Memphis. Upon my arrival in Memphis, my father picked me up at the airport and checked me into a hotel. The following morning I went to work with my father at Beathan Trading. This gave me a firsthand look at Beathan Trading's operations and money raising.

Later that day, Max Beathan called me into his office. I was granted an audience with Max.

I walked into Max's office at Beathan Trading. He greeted me and told me to have a seat in front of his desk. We both sat down. He told me he had arranged an interview with REFCO in Chicago. This was Treston Lakeman's huge clearinghouse on the CME. Max told me that REFCO had an excellent training program for a young man like myself. We shook hands, and I thanked him for the opportunity. We walked out of his office onto the clearing floor of Beathan Trading, and Max introduced me to Peter Copperman and Scott Maison. We chatted for a while.

To celebrate my interview in Chicago, Peter and Scott invited me out for a night on the town. This was quite an evening. Prior to this evening, I had been clean of drugs for two months.

The evening consisted of going to nightclubs and the home of a customer of Beathan Trading. At the customer's home, Scott encouraged me to do bong hits of marijuana, with Peter Copperman's approval. After we left the customer's home, Peter left. But Scott had more damage to do. Scott asked me to go to a strip joint, and I was stupid enough to go along, thinking I had a new friend. When we got in his car, he whipped out a baggy of cocaine, and we proceeded to snort it. All the while, Scott kept saying, "Your dad and Max don't need to know what we do."

We pulled into a gas station for some fuel, and I got out and puked. The cocaine was obviously laced with speed, which I cannot tolerate. Finally, we went to the strip joint, Danny's. The evening ended, and Scott drove me back to the hotel.

Now, I'll let you in on what Scott and Peter Copperman were up to. Peter Copperman's little brother, Alan, was Beathan's filling broker in the live cattle pit on the CME (Chicago Mercantile Exchange) floor, and Peter did not want any competition for his little brother. If I were successfully trained to be a filling broker by REFCO, I might pose a threat to Alan's income and business. They successfully loaded me up with marijuana, cocaine, and speed three days prior to my REFCO interview, knowing full well there was a drug test for employment. IT'S A CUTTHROAT WORLD IN THE COMMODITIES BUSINESS!! And I was a SUCKER!!

The following morning, my father woke me up at the hotel and informed me that in addition to the REFCO interview, he had also arranged a second interview with LIT America through his old friend Dan O'Connor, a cattle business associate.

Do you suppose that my dad and Max knew about the Experiment at this point? I hope not. I do not believe so. But, again, I could have been set up from the get-go.

I flew to Chicago, excited about the prospect of entering into the commodities business.

CHAPTER 4

Knocking on Chicago's Door

In mid-November of 1990, I flew into Chicago' O'Hare airport and caught a cab to Nathan Baxter's parents' house. Nathan was a good friend and frat brother from the University of Wisconsin. We had a good time hanging out in Chicago the night I arrived.

The following morning, I caught another cab, to REFCO's home office at the Board of Trade. I was to meet with Mr. Fairchild, Treston Lakeman's right-hand man, because Mr. Lakeman was in the Orient. I sat outside Mr. Fairchild's office door reading the *Wall Street Journal*, patiently waiting for the interview. Mr. Fairchild greeted me, and we stepped into his office. He began with normal questions about my life and then asked about my commodities background. Things were running smoothly, when he asked if I had a problem with a drug policy. Somewhat concerned, I replied that I did not have a problem with a drug policy. He then said, "Good. You need to take a urine test."

I was trapped. Many companies had drug policies but did not

require pre-employment drug tests. That was why I responded that I did not have a problem with a drug policy. Somewhat panicked, I said, "I do not have any ID with me." Mr. Fairchild smiled and said that I did not need one and began to tell me where to go for the drug test. I was trying to think of someone in Chicago who was clean who could take the drug test for me. There was no time! My mind was a blank. What could I say? I thought to myself. I asked if I could take the test in three weeks, when I returned for the job.

"Why?" Mr. Fairchild asked.

Now I had no out. I thought I'd come clean and lie. Another rookie mistake.

"Well, to be honest, I went to a reggae concert last night and took a drag off a marijuana cigarette."

"After admitting that to me, you will be unable to work here at REFCO," Mr. Fairchild firmly said.

My heart dropped as part of my possible future disappeared. I stood up and thanked Mr. Fairchild for his time and left the room.

I took the elevator to the ground floor of the Board of Trade. I was very stressed out. What do I do now? I asked myself. I walked over to the store inside the Board and bought a pack of smokes. I went outside and walked around the Board of Trade building four times and power smoked. The cigarettes offered some relief.

So I walked back inside and went to a pay phone to call my father with the terrible news. Naturally, he went berserk. I asked him if I should go see Dan O'Connor, executive vice president of Prudential Securities in charge of all commodities operations in Chicago, an old family friend. My father had given Mr. O'Connor a lot of live cattle contract business over the years, when my father was running packing plants (Cargill and Val-Agra).

My father responded, "Well, yes, Billy, that's all you have left. Do you realize that you have cut your chances of becoming a broker by half?" Then I asked my father, "Do you want me to tell Max, or would you like to?" "Yes, you call back and tell Max what happened."

So I called Max and stuck to the same marijuana cigarette lie. This must have been an embarrassment to my father.

Max was a little too nice on the phone. He said, "Just be cool, Billy. Maybe you can still work for REFCO."

Was this all a setup, or were Scott's and Peter Copperman's actions independent of my father and Max? I still do not know. My father later informed me that Treston Lakeman and Max had a fight over me. Nevertheless, I did not receive a job offer from REFCO either. Strike two!

I went outside and smoked some more. I gathered myself and got ready to meet Dan for the first time. I did not know it at the time, but I was going to meet a friend, free of setups, and one of my mentors at the Merc!!!

I took the elevator up to the Prudential Securities back office and asked the secretary to see Mr. O'Connor. She inquired as to whom I was. "Billy Nicholson." She stuck her head inside Dan's door and then told me to go into his office. Dan was standing behind his desk, and the first thing he said to me was "You must take after your mother's side of the family, with a nice suit and a full head of hair."

Dan sat down and began to inquire about my interview with REFCO. I did not reveal the problem. He then said, "Billy, the only problem with working for REFCO is everyone will be more concerned with what your father and Beathan Trading are doing than in having an interest in you!" "I agree, Mr. O'Connor. Tell me what LIT America has to offer," I replied. Dan looked a little puzzled. "Call me Dan, Billy."

"Well, LIT can train you from the ground up, and in a few years, you may be very useful to them," Dan explained. What Dan knew that I did not know was LIT America would be bought out in the near future. Dan picked up the phone and arranged an immediate interview with LIT America. We continued to have a pleasant conversation, and then Dan said, "I need to get back to work." Dan said as we got up from our seats, "Good luck with your interview. If anyone asks you for a reference, use the name Henry Bandoni." I thanked Dan profusely for providing me with the opportunity.

Later that afternoon, I went to the LIT office, also at the Board of Trade, and interviewed with a nice personnel woman. She asked me why I wanted to work for LIT. "We do not have many interviews with people as sharp as you and as well dressed." (I was overqualified was the gist of her conversation.) I informed her that I wanted to learn the business from the ground up, starting as a runner. She was very complimentary and said she would let me know.

Finally, the day was coming to a close. The stress was easing off. Nathan Baxter's parents were having a party that night, so I checked into a hotel. With my pride totally crushed, I called LIT to inform them where I could be contacted.

My good friend Nathan stopped by and tried to talk me into going to a reggae concert. We had planned to go that night, not the previous night. That was why my lie had been so easy and natural. Despite Nathan's best efforts to get me to go the concert, I declined.

Nathan left my hotel room, and shortly after, the phone rang.

It was LIT America offering me a job beginning on December 1.

Third time at bat, and I finally landed a job with a lot of help from Dan and Henry. You will learn more about Henry Bandoni later in this book and my natural progression toward going to work for him.

I flew home to Wichita the following morning.

CHAPTER 5

My Exit from Wichita

I returned to Wichita during the week. My mother was excited that I had a job lined up in Chicago. We did not have to deal with my father until the next weekend.

My father was digging himself out of a hole. He had a negative net worth. He had gone more than broke by trading cattle and losing his job as president of Val-Agra, a cattle-packing company. Val-Agra was a company he started, financed by a wealthy businessman out of Dallas. My father lost his position as head of Val-Agra when the company merged into Swift Independent to save it from going under. This wealthy Texas businessman did, however, pay out the remainder of my father's contract. So my father did have this income, and he was successfully trading cattle for Max Beathan, who was kind enough to give him a job. My family had already lost our house in Aspen to the bank, and the Wichita house was on the market. My father made an agreement with the bank, First Oklahoma City, to pay them back over time and not declare bankruptcy. Which he eventually did. But he drank heavily and was a real bastard in these days. My father's financial status was a well-kept secret.

I broke the harsh news to Marshall Clarkstone, owner of Brick's. I told him I was beginning employment in Chicago December 1 and would not be able to work through the end of the busy retail season. He did know that I was interviewing during November, but he did not yet know my start date. Basically, I left him shorthanded going into the busiest time of year, Christmas and Hanukah.

Marshall was very kind and said, "If your mind is made up, I will not offer you the increased commission level for 1991." Marshall had plans for me and my ability to sell clothes. I think he did not expect me to stick around forever, but maybe a year or so. If I had just waited a month and a half to go to Chicago, I would have gone with a lot more money in my pocket. I also would have helped Marshall out if I had started around January 10.

Nevertheless, Marshall wished me the best, and we parted as friends.

Then the weekend came and brought my father with it. He was steamed. The first thing he said, walking into the house, was "Do you realize that Max and Treston Lakeman got into a fight over you!!" The disgust was written all over his flushed, red face.

"Dad, I will get a good education from LIT America, according to Dan," I countered.

"Billy, REFCO is the largest brokerage group on the floor at the Merc. Getting a brokerage position is very difficult without help," he vented.

I began packing my bags for Chicago. The question of whether or not I was going to take my car to Chicago was still up in the air. I checked into the cost of insuring a 2002 BMW in Chicago. Naturally, Chicago was an expensive place to insure a car. This fact, coupled with my driving record, made the possibility of moving to Chicago and taking my car cost prohibitive. Or at least that was my father's opinion after I told him the insurance quote.

"Why do you need a car in Chicago anyway? The mass transit system is very good and inexpensive," my father replied. He was dead set against me taking my car to Chicago. It was OK to pay for my plane ticket, security deposit on my apartment, and furnishings for my apartment but not for insurance on my car, and he insisted that I sell it before my departure. Therefore, I had less than a week to sell it.

Thankfully, Terry Hammond, manager of Brick's, offered to take it off my hands for the discount price of five hundred dollars. He turned right around and sold it for more money. But I did not have time to properly sell it for full value, and it solved the problem.

Finally, almost everything was going my way, with the exception of the car. I packed everything that would fit into my suitcases. I was ready to go.

My father cooled off by the end of the weekend and wished me luck in Chicago as he boarded a plane back to Memphis. My mother and I went back home after my father's departure and organized my move to Chicago as much as possible.

At the end of November, I flew to Chicago. My mother shortly followed me to Chicago and helped me find an apartment at 1100 North Dearborn. My mother is an interior designer, ASID, and she furnished my apartment for me.

CHAPTER **6**

Getting into the Exchange

Riding up the escalator for the first time to be an employee on the Merc exchange floor, I realized that despite my initial problems to find employment in the commodities business, I was actually going to work on the floor. I walked up to the paging desk at the top of the escalator and asked for Jake Russo, floor manager for LIT. I waited a long time, and Jake finally came out and introduced himself. We walked onto the Merc floor at 30 South Wacker. Jake took me over to the S & P desk and told me to just stand on the lower steps for a while. Organized chaos.

For the first time I watched the runners take paper from the phone desk to the S & P pit. The phone clerks were perched on step stools on the highest steps of the phone order bays of LIT's operation. These clerks were receiving both at-the-market orders and orders above and below the market. The orders that were not at-the-market were handwritten and given to the runners to take to the pit. Market orders or ones near the market were also handwritten, but the phone clerks used arb signals (hand signals) to the clerks standing at the edge of the pit. The pit clerks would then turn to the brokers in the pit and tell them to execute the orders. Once completed, the pit clerks would again send arb signals back to the phone clerks, and they would tell the customers on the phone the filling prices and quantities, and the phone clerks would also write the information on the paper orders. The broker in the pit would fill out cards with this same information and give it to the pit clerk. Then it was the responsibility of the runner to pick up the cards and filled paper orders at the pit and return them to LIT's desk, for the phone clerks. The phone clerks would then match the cards to the paper orders of the at-the-market orders and call the customers back to report the fill of the paper-filled orders.

I traded commodities in college, and my father had me looking at market charts and managing his commodity trades on my first computer, as a child, an Apple II Plus. So, figuring out the floor was fairly simple for me.

Jake was standing with his back to me. He then turned around and said, "Henry Bandoni sent you to us, right?" "That's correct," I replied. "OK, go up to compliance and get your photo ID and jacket," Jake instructed.

So I went to compliance and got my photo ID, and then they sent me to the third floor to get my yellow floor jacket. I returned to the S & P desk. Jake told me to be a runner in the S & P for the rest of the day. It was a blast. After a few hours, Jake and his right-hand man, Curtis, returned and asked me what I wanted to do on the floor. I replied, "I want to be a runner in one of the currencies, preferably the Swiss or Dmark." Curtis and Jake looked at each other and said, "Dmark." Curtis then said to me, "You don't want to work in the Swiss, kid—it sucks." Jake then told me that Curtis would take me over to the Dmark and show me where it was and to report the next morning at 7:00 a.m. Curtis took me over to the Dmark desk and introduced me to the desk manager, Brad.

I was on cloud nine. The Dmark! I love Germans and German products and German money.

CHAPTER 7

Being a Runner at the Dmark Desk

I reached the exchange the next morning at 6:30 a.m. and reported to the Dmark desk at 6:45 a.m. Brad was already there. The rest of the crew filed in at 7:00.

I met Chris, Quitin, and Travis. Chris was a large individual, who eventually went to work for FIMAT (Society General, a large French bank) as a phone clerk in the Dmark. FIMAT would eventually give him an Exchange seat and a front-row desk to trade the arbitrage. But, this happened long after I left LIT. Quitin was a very bright trader, who would leave the LIT desk to take a rice seat and trade using his own money at the Board of Trade. Quitin would leave while I was still working for LIT. Travis was a Schaumburg kid and was always half-asleep and strung out from the night before. He did not last.

All of these guys were great to me and thoroughly explained my duties as a runner. They informed me I should always inspect the orders before I ran them to the pit. I was to check for a time stamp, quantity, and price. They said the order should also have an account number at the top right-hand corner and should be legibly clear as a buy or sell order, written either on the left or right side of the order. They also informed me to pay attention to the contract month, which determined to which brokerage group the order was to be taken. Spreads were a little more complicated—they had information written on both sides of the order. Quantities were always the same, but they could have a price on both sides of the order or one in the middle.

Then they explained that for the front month we used FB Trading, a brokerage group at the front of the pit, and Alfred Mallikin in the back of the pit for all months that were not the front-month contracts.

Then Brad took me down to meet Tess, point clerk, for FB Trading. FB Trading (Felix Bienkowski Trading) was a division of ABS (Associated Brokerage Services). Tess was very kind and always helped me out with any problems. Tess introduced me to Zach and Martin, the deck holders. These were the guys I was to give my paper orders from the desk. The deck consisted of all the orders with whom FB Trading had business arrangements divided into buy and sell orders (the two sides of the deck) and then placed in order by price. Tess also introduced me to Big Ben, a heavyset Greek kid, who received arb phone signals from our desk and Lind Waldock. In addition to running paper, I would be responsible for picking up filled paper orders from Zach and Martin and cards from Big Ben, as I explained in the last chapter.

After these introductions, Brad took me to the back of the pit and introduced me to Alfred Mallikin. Alfred did not have a clerk, except during rollover. He was very nice. Alfred would receive all back-month orders and spreads, except during rollover, when we divided the spreads between FB Trading and himself.

Rollover is when the front-month contract is expiring or going of the board. Futures contracts have a limited number of days of existence, and if you do not go from the front month to one of the back months using a spread or market orders at expiration, the future will be exercised. This means you would take delivery of the commodity—in this case, cash Deutschmarks.

I ran for about a month and got to know the brokers in the FB Trading group quite well. There were Felix Bienkowski, of course, and his brother, Jay; Dale Patras, who was the big brother of Zach, the deck holder; Donnie Stoat; Kevin Hisakawa; and Howard Neiland.

The Dmark pit was set up similar to the S & P pit, octangular with three steps down into a large open area. The filling brokers stood on the steps, and the locals stood in the open area. Naturally, the front-month brokers stood along the front of the pit, and the back-month brokers stood along the back of the pit. The pit recorder, an employee of the exchange, was between the front and back, just to the right of FB Trading's brokerage group.

The duty of the pit recorder was to type in trading price and quantity (volume) as it occurred. This information would appear on the electronic boards on the walls of the exchange and on the screens of people trading off the floor. The exchange gathered this information at time and sales off the floor and matched it against each clearinghouse's off-floor operations.

Between each pit on the floor and the phone bays was a narrow walkway. Then the phone bays began.

In the Dmark, the arbitrage traders or the banks stood on the same level as the walkway, facing the pit, with their phones behind them. Then there were three tiers of phones after that. LIT's desk was on the highest tier, and all of my phone clerks stood on step stools facing our phones and the pit.

CHAPTER **8**

Living Blissfully in Chicago

I loved my apartment at 1100 North Dearborn. It was built in the 1920s. It was a bit of a shoebox and had window air-conditioning. But it had parquet wood floors, radiator steam heat, a built-in bookshelf, a gas stove with a broiler, and a walk-in closet to the bathroom. The bathroom had an old freestanding porcelain tub with a showerhead coming out of the wall above and a wraparound shower curtain. There was an old wooden window next to the tub. The sink was also freestanding and porcelain with a wonderful old medicine cabinet. The floor was old white tile. All the walls and wood trim in the apartment were whitewashed. I lived on the third floor. The lobby was art deco with incredible woodwork and 1920s vintage furniture. There was a twenty-four-hour doorman at a double entrance and an entrance phone to the front desk. The doorman would then call me on my house phone in my apartment and announce arrivals. I had both a private line and house phone. It was really convenient to have people wait in the lobby and just come down and meet them. I was a closet habitual marijuana smoker. I never went stoned to work, but when the bell rang at 2:00 p.m. in the Dmark, I was headed home to toke and relax.

A lot of my college frat brothers from the University of Wisconsin had moved to Chicago, and I had an instant network of friends. Just like when I jumped from college to college, good old Sigma Chi helped me here too. Clyde Wrighte was a frat bother who worked on the floor, and Nathan Baxter would come for regular visits. Then, one day after I had been working at the exchange for about six months, I received a call on the house phone, and the doorman said, "Barry Martin is here with a large bag and wants to come up. Do you know him?" I replied, "Yes, send him up." The doorman asked, "What's in the bag?" I said, "If it makes you nervous, ask him to let you look in it." He said OK and did.

I had a queen bed and a futon couch that converted into bed in the main room, so Barry moved in for two months. We had a great time on Rush Street, which was just around the corner from my place, and the Dearborn Social Club and Zebra Lounge, but mostly we smoked pot. Finally, I came home one afternoon and threw a newspaper at Barry and said, "Get a job." He took the hint and got an old Brownstone up in Wrigleyville for himself. Later I would move in there, with him this time.

In addition to friends my own age, Dan O'Connor turned out to be a great friend and mentor. He gave me the number to his private, untaped phone line at work, and we had breakfast at the best restaurant at the Board of Trade at least once a month. I could contact him anytime and ask him anything. I was very careful to never bother him at home, to keep the relationship somewhat professional.

Now, let us backtrack to my transition from runner to phone clerk at the exchange.

CHAPTER 9

Being a Phone Clerk for LIT

Chris was my best friend at the Dmark desk. Sometimes after work we would go get high, but never very often.

While I was running, Chris coached me on how to be a phone clerk. He taught me never take an order without first getting an account number. The proper way to answer the phone was "Dmark what's your account number?" From there, the customers would give an order near the market, at-the-market, or above or below. Basically, there are market orders (buy or sell at the market), limit orders (at a specific price), and stops (buy stops go above the market and sell stops go below the market).

After receiving an account number, the customer might say, "Buy one March Dmark" or "Sell one March Dmark." This was the easiest. Or they might ask, "What's in the front month?" and you would quote them, and they would give you a limit order. After most orders, they would also give you a stop order, which you sent in on paper. Stops are for suckers and people without much money. There is a time to get in and a time to get out, in my opinion. Most of what Chris told me I already knew. But Chris letting me listen as he took orders and watch what he wrote down was a big help! Everyone at the desk taught me the arb signals, but Chris was the best teacher, followed closely by Brad. Once you had the basic signals down, you could stand and watch the activity between the phones and the pit to learn the rest.

Finally, one day, Chris said, "Do you want to try one?" I did everything correctly but wrote the order on the wrong side. I committed a buy-sell error my first time out. Did I mention that I am dyslexic? I was trained by the Catholic nuns at Kansas Newman College in Wichita, Kansas, as a child to overcome it. I never made another dyslexic error at the exchange again.

When I completed the order and received the arb signal from the pit, I said, "You paid seventy-eight on one March Dmark." The customer said in a very calm voice that it was supposed to be a sell order. (Thank god he was a nice guy.) I was horrified and handed the order and phone to Chris and said, "It's a sell order." Chris grinned, yelled for Tess in the pit, and lifted up his tie (the signal for being hung). He glanced at me, and from the expression on my face, Tess knew I was hung. Chris arbed in two at eight. The market had already moved. Tess leaned into Felix and arbed back two at eight. That's how the floor worked—we took care of each other!!!! Then Chris called Jake and told him I had a buy-sell error. He scratched it, and the customer was satisfied. Jake told him to have me run the rest of the day.

The next morning I reported to the desk at 6:45, and Brad was all grins. He said, "You're on the phones now. Jake listened to the tape and liked your style. There's a trick you should know, Bill: as soon as they say buy or sell, mark through *Buy* or *Sell*, which is printed on the order." I was flawless after that.

Big Ben was the arb clerk responsible for LIT and Lind Waldock for FB Trading. We became good friends from the start. He was so superior to Martin, it was ridiculous. Most of the time Martin held half the deck with Zach. But, sometimes Martin was the arb clerk, he would hang both desks out to dry, and brokers too, all the time. When Big Mike was on break or sick, everyone was nervous.

Our desk would usually handle small orders with some tens, twenties, and hundred lots mixed in, but one account was large, New Bridge International out of White Plains, New York. Everyone took pride in handling their business, which came in between a thousand and fifteen hundred lots. They were market or limit orders with no stops.

Remember what I said about stops? New Bridge International had deep pockets. We sent these orders in on paper to Tess and told the runner to have her look at the phone clerk executing so no one picked us off. Tess would then arb the fills out to us as they came in. Tess of course did ask the bank broker's phone clerk nearest to the filling broker for a bid or offer depending on whether it was a sell or a buy order. Some people think this is giving up the edge. But the Dmark's locals were not large or numerous enough to provide enough liquidity to fill this large an order. So giving up a few points to the cash arbitrage traders or banks was doing the customer a favor and yielded a better fill.

I spent five months as a phone clerk in the Dmark. During that time, Jake Russo got replaced as floor manager by Jonas Mattox. Prior to Jake's departure, Curtis came to me in private and told me there were going to be some changes in LIT and that I should not tell anyone that Henry Bandoni got me my job at the company. This made me nervous, and I left the floor and called Dan on his private line at a pay phone two buildings away from the Merc. Dan told me not to worry about it and said Curtis was trying to get a piece of me, but it was good advice.

Then, one morning at breakfast with Dan, he told me, "Billy, if you can ever do a large favor for someone without really doing anything, do it, but never break the law on the floor."

A month later, my chance came with Jonas Mattox at the helm. Priscilla from New Bridge International called before the open, and I answered the phone. She gave me two very large sell orders at the market, one in the front month and one in the back month. She also told me that the broker could work the orders. So I asked, "You're giving discretion on these orders, right?" She answered, "Yes." I then inquired, "Would you like Felix to fill both orders?" She answered, "If he likes." The bitch took the bait. So I filled out both orders and went down to Felix three minutes before the bell and said, "Felix, Priscilla said you can fill both of these orders and work them. I confirmed that they are discretionary orders." Felix took both orders and thanked me. I had done nothing wrong and

opened the door for Felix. Felix and Priscilla had spoken regularly on our taped line at the LIT Dmark desk. As I walked
away, I watched Felix show both orders to his brother, Jay.
When I was perched back at my desk, I watched Felix yell
across the pit to Alfred Mallikin in the back month and arb an
order to him. Now, Jay was allowed to trade his own account
either for himself or for his brother, and Felix was allowed to
trade his own account through any other broker.

The bell rang, and Jay banged out a large order or trade with
all the banks; Alfred Mallikin was busy doing the same. Both
Jay and Alfred were done in thirty seconds, and it was selling
down the market. Then Felix started with all the locals in the
front month, and the market was headed south. Just before the
end of the opening range, Felix stepped out into the middle
of the pit and executed the back-month order to all the back-
month locals. He finished up two minutes later.

What I got back was two terribly filled orders. I made Brad call
back the fills to Priscilla. I told him I was busy on the phone
with another customer; remember, these orders went in on
paper before the open so anyone could call them back. Also
remember that I was on a taped line with Priscilla. Mission
accomplished, and I challenge anyone to prove any wrong-
doing at this late date.

The next morning, Jonas Mattox called me into his office with
his two henchmen, Derek and Roy, for a "hot box." He asked,
"What did you tell the filling broker about the two orders you
got from New Bridge International yesterday?" Very innocently,
I said, "Priscilla told me that he could fill both orders and they

were discretionary." Jonas Mattox said, "Well, Bill, after a lot of discussion and thought, we have decided not to fire you!!!" Then Roy, one of Jonas's henchmen, said, "Bill, when I heard you ask if one broker could fill both orders, I knew there was going to be a problem. That's why we have a front- and a back-month broker." I replied, "I'm SORRY." Then Jonas lectured me for about an hour and said, "With what you said to the filling broker, I cannot go to him and ask for an adjustment on these orders. Do you know that first I agreed to adjust the front month for the customer? Then he called me back and said, 'If you adjusted the front month, how can you not adjust the back month.' So I had to adjust that too." We all stood up and I again apologized and shook Jonas's hand and left and went back to work.

I waited a few hours until the market died down and then went to the pit to talk to Felix. I asked, "Felix can I speak to you in private?" He responded, "Sure." We walked over to the edge of the stairs going up to the phones and Felix said, "What can I help you with, Bill?" I then said, "If anyone comes to talk to you about those two big orders for New Bridge from yesterday, tell them I told you that you could fill both orders and they were discretionary, because that is the truth, and that is also what I told Jonas Mattox this morning." Felix quickly said, "OK, Bill," and we both went back to work. At the end of the day, I waited for everyone to leave the desk and pulled the dupes (paper copies of an order) from the previous day on these New Bridge orders and kept them in the inside pocket of my yellow coat for insurance.

Therefore, the customer, New Bridge International, did not get hurt any after the adjustments, but it did not do LIT's error account much good.

A week later, the head of LIT came to visit me. He walked up the steps to the desk, with Jonas Mattox following sheepishly and Derek and Roy in tow, and tapped me on the shoulder. "Son, we have not met, but I believe we have a mutual friend, Dan O'Connor." I replied, "Yes, sir, he is a close family friend." He then said, "I think you'll find we have the same friends." Jonas Mattox, from some distance away, said somewhat apologetically, "I did not know that." Then the head of LIT stood on the step stool next to me, facing the pit, and we proceeded to have a pleasant conversation.

After he left, Brad turned to me and said, "That was a very impressive guest you had come visit you, Bill, wasn't it?" I said, "I guess so."

The next time I had breakfast with Dan, I thanked him for sending the head of LIT to meet me on the floor. Dan said, "No problem, Billy. He's quite a nice guy, but one of the goofiest bastards I have ever met."

I proceeded to be a star as a phone clerk in the Dmark after that. Big Ben kindled our relationship.

Little did I know I was going to be trained by Dustin Knox and moved to the Euro dollars to be the one-man desk manager of small business.

CHAPTER 10

My Relationship with Big Ben

Ben Kallas was a member of the Fiji fraternity at the University of Wisconsin and knew many of my fraternity brothers, including Barry Martin, but I never met him at Wisconsin. So we hit it off from the start.

One day after working in the Dmark, he invited me over to his place on North Belmont. We arrived around 3:00 p.m. at his place and got high. We spent the afternoon reminiscing about Madison and what a fun campus it was. At 5:30 p.m., his roommate, Jason Garret, came home. Jason had his series three registration and was an off-floor commodity broker for Ira Epstein. Jason, Ben, and I sat out on their back deck and discussed the commodities markets. Periodically, Ben and I would go into the apartment to smoke and gain back our buzz, only to return to the deck and to the discussion.

As time went on, Ben informed me that his father was a restaurateur in Lake Geneva, Wisconsin, where Ben had grown up. I told Ben my father's background was in cattle and that he now worked for Beathan Trading in Memphis, Tennessee.

I never volunteered to Ben or anyone information about my father's financial condition or the difficulty I had getting into the commodities business.

Ben was basically the only one off the floor whom I regularly socialized with. He also was my weed connection. The floor was the "candy store," and scoring weed there was no problem, but out of professionalism I always got mine elsewhere. Ben knew plenty of off-floor connections. I'm sure Ben made a lot of money off me.

We had similar taste in music and interests. We ate out at restaurants in his neighborhood, and when he came to my place, we did the same. But we were new floor clerks, which meant low income, so we mostly hung out, got high, and talked shop.

We basically were together all day at work and spent three to four days a week together outside work.

Ben and I started hanging out with Barry at his place at 3828 North Sheffield in Wrigleyville. It was an old brownstone, and he had the entire second floor. Barry, Ben, and I smoked pot together and played hard in Wrigleyville. My favorite bar was Murphy's, across from the ballpark, which had great bar food and Guinness on tap and a great scotch selection.

The El ride home was sketchy at night and a cab ride was expensive. So Barry suggested that I move in. The El stop was less than a block away, and the ride down to the Merc was only about ten minutes longer than from 1100 North Dearborn. All my friends lived in Wrigleyville or Lincoln Park; therefore, this location was more socially ideal.

The leasing agent at 1100 North Dearborn assured me that she could sublet my apartment. So I made the move.

Barry made me a great deal of three hundred dollars a month, and I got the back bedroom. At that time, he had a roommate, Wade. The three of us had a great time together. Then Wade moved out after a few months, and Matt Pagani, a friend of Ben's from Lake Geneva, moved in.

Matt was a great guy, but he started dealing drugs out of the apartment. Matt was a very sloppy dealer.

I did not like the risk and exposure that Matt was posing for me.

Then Nathan Baxter got a two-bedroom apartment on West Waveland, just down the street from Murphy's, and asked me to move in with him. Barry bid me farewell, and I moved in with Nathan.

Nathan was my favorite frat brother from Wisconsin. He was a struggling guitarist and musician. Nathan could play the guitar better than anyone I had ever met.

Nathan was also very intellectual, and the conversations we had while getting high were far superior to my other friends' conversations. We never talked about the exchange, and I had plenty of other friends to talk shop with.

Then Trent Seaton, my pledge son and Nathan's roommate in the fraternity house at Wisconsin, came to stay with us and slept on the couch. Trent was also very intellectual. The three of us would hang out get high and talk while Nathan would play the guitar.

I got Trent a job on the floor with LIT, and he lasted two days, because Kegan Lowrance, a friend I had gained through Beathan Trading offered me a job with his brokerage group in the Euros. I declined and suggested that I had a friend who would make an excellent clerk and might want the job. He hired Trent. Kegan Lowrance was a really nice guy, but he was a silver-spooner from Memphis who got a seat on the floor with his family money the day he walked on the floor and traded for himself. I think he thought I was rich too.

I told Trent he could stay with us as long as he liked, and he stayed quite a while and then moved out and got an apartment with a Board of Trade clerk.

I still spent a lot of time with Matt and Barry; my apartment with Nathan was only three blocks away from Barry's place. Matt had connections on the floor with a Euro-dollar brokerage firm in the pit, and I suggested that he take a job with them. And he did.

Occasionally I would hang out with Clyde Wrighte in Lincoln Park and all of his friends.

So, my social life was pretty good.

CHAPTER 11

The Euro Dollars

While I was still working as a phone clerk in the Dmark, Jonas Mattox arranged for me to be trained in Euro-dollar operations by Dustin Knox. The Euros are complex. Ted spreads, regular spreads, butterflies, and iron butterflies, just to name a few. Dustin did an excellent job of training me, but my real love was still the Dmarks.

LIT's plan was to have me replace Dustin in the Euros but I did not know this, and I'm not sure Dustin knew either. Dustin was a great guy and even took me to a White Sox baseball game with excellent seats. I think LIT believed he was being paid too much money for his position, considering what little work he was doing. This one-man desk was not very busy, and LIT was trimming the fat after the buyout.

One day I took the dupes from the New Bridge fill out of my inside pocket and said, "What happened here?" as I showed them to Dustin. His response was "They could have done a better job of filling them." After he looked at them, I put the dupes back in my inside pocket. I do not know if he told anybody about them, but if he did, it could have been the kiss of death.

I did not like that LIT canned Dustin after he trained me, and I really never liked the Euros. I was a real greenhorn at the desk.

I befriended the two ladies who worked the high-volume desk for LIT right next to me. They were handling Goldman Sack's account. I even went so far as to ask for a job and interviewed with the one in charge.

On the other side of my desk was Bank of Japan. I also became good friends with them too.

I really did not like the Euros very much—too confusing and difficult with narrow ranges (the prices between the high and low of a trading day), and people were trading for a couple of ticks. Quite unlike the currencies, which had huge ranges. I concluded that the easy money and easy work were back in the Dmark, even though the Euros had almost triple the volume (the number of contracts traded in a day).

So I told the head guy at Bank of Japan, who had half a desk and three brokers, that I really did not mind if he took my desk space. He said, "If you really don't mind, I'll take it," and did. They threw me away into a corner desk up by the spreads.

Then the head man from Bank of Japan came up to me and pointed out that there was a full desk space right behind him, and I took that. Therefore, I did another simple favor without doing anything.

Then, I went back to the Dmark and asked Felix for a job in the pit with him. He offered me one. I told him I would need to give my two weeks with LIT and would like to go on vacation first.

I also inquired again with Goldman Sacks, and they told me I was a strong candidate.

So I called Dan and told him I had two job offers. When I told him a woman was running Goldman Sacks, he replied, "Billy, a woman on the floor being in charge is kind of bad, but Goldman doesn't care about their fill price—they just want them. However, if you go to work with ABS, I can control your future, and you will learn everything, including how to steal." "Well, should I wait to see who comes with the best offer?" I queried. "No, you do not do that on the floor, Billy," Dan counseled. I then said, "I want to work for Felix." "Great," Dan said. "Tell Goldman you are going to work for ABS because you owe them," and then he laughed.

So I declined with Goldman. Put in my two weeks with LIT. Negotiated my pay with Felix. And flew to Jamaica for a week.

The real tragedies with my three months in the Euros are I did not really like it and Dustin Knox lost his job. I do not know if Dustin would have lost it anyway.

CHAPTER 12

Working for ABS

After returning from Jamaica, I went to work for FB Trading. This meant I was working for ABS and Henry Bandoni. Henry became my mentor along with Dan. On the floor, I was Felix Bienkowski's boy.

I began by holding the deck but quickly became an arb clerk along with Big Ben. I watched LIT and Ben handled Lind Waldock. I mainly worked with filling brokers Kevin Hisakawa and Donnie Stoat in the beginning. I was flawless and never made errors.

When Ben chose to leave the floor to take a vacation in the Caribbean and never came back, I basically stole his job from him. He could have stuck around, and we could have later been filling brokers together. He was somewhat blessed, but I held all the cards with Prudential and LIT's business liking me. This was the bulk of FB Trading's and ABS's business.

Prior to his departure, when we were off the floor, in private Ben would always point out the corruption of ABS and say,

"Who do we work for, Bill, the Mob?" He took me up to Lake Geneva and painted the picture of his father being a restaurateur with Mob ties. Ben was kind of a scumbag.

After Ben left, I handled both the Lind Waldock and the LIT desks. It was a barrage of one lots with some larger business mixed in. I never hung any of my brokers and took excellent care of my desks; I was error-free. I was a star in this position. The Dmark would have ranges of around eighty points a day, and I would process thousands of orders daily. I loved the action.

Except, one day, just before Ben left, I was working the point, watching Prudential's desk, and I did not know that Lind Waldock also had another desk below Prudential's and occasionally placed orders with us. Ben pointed him out to me. With sloppy arb signals the clerk sent in a ten lot, which I checked with him three times as a hundred lot; he shook his head and confirmed it. I gave the order to Jay. The market was dead, and he had to bid it up to fill a hundred lot. Once Jay finished, I arbed back the fill. The clerk came to the pit, looked at the card, and said, "It is supposed to be a ten lot." I told Jay that I checked the order three times, but it was a ten-versus-hundred-lot error. Jay worked the market and got out with a five-thousand-dollar loss and then turned to Ben, who was laughing, and said, "You were supposed to be watching him too." Ben watched the whole thing and offered no help—kind of a jerk, wouldn't you say? This was my only error with FB Trading, and it was a negligible loss.

With Ben out of the picture, I could work any house with

precision.

Then about a month later, Tess made a fifty-lot error with one of the banks on a blow-off volume and huge-range day. She and Felix did not figure it out until the end of the day. She confirmed and gave a fill on a fifty lot that Felix never executed. Felix had to get out in the EFPs (exchange for physical, or after-hours cash market). This was a monstrously expensive error.

They replaced Tess with Sidney. Sidney was a past broker at SDS who had returned as a clerk after the merger of ABS and SDS, which became International Futures and Options. Sidney was the new point man and a good clerk.

Then one day I went to work, and halfway through the day, I told Felix that it was my birthday. He left the pit, stepped up to one of the phones, made a call, and left.

Then everyone left, except for Kevin and Donnie. Then Rick Pagani, who worked the group occasionally, arrived. Sidney, who was all smiles, said, "Bill, you work the point for a while." Kevin got the deck, and Donnie and Rick stood next to me, facing the pit. The desk manager of Prudential signaled me and mouthed, "Watch me," and pointed to himself. He stepped to the corner in the back of the desk with orders in his hand. Prudential's floor manager was standing next to him. He proceeded to arb in cross orders in hundred lots at a specific price. I turned to the pit and said, "Donnie, six on a hundred." Donnie bid them out to the pit (open outcry), and as soon as he was done, I said, "Rick, sell 'em." Rick said,

"Sold into the pit" (open outcry). Then the Prudential clerk arbed in a hundred-lot sell and then a buy at a specific price. I started with Rick this time, and we did it in reverse. We banged off about a thousand crosses with open outcry, and we were done. I did everything perfectly. The Prudential floor manager, halfway through, turned to the desk manager and asked, "How's he doing?" "Great," the desk manager replied with a smile. You get really good at reading lips when you are working on the floor.

Then Sidney, after I was done, said, "I bet you wish you could do that all the time." And smiled. "Back to the one lots." I went back to watching LIT and Lind Waldock.

I enjoyed this, but it made me a little nervous. What I found out later was block trading, crossing orders, and laundry all look the same, and the pit clerks and pit brokers cannot get into any legal trouble, as long as open outcry (offering to the pit) is used. The people on the outside of the floor, placing the orders, were the ones at risk!!!

Because I was a little nervous, I called my father and asked to come home and talk to him. Two weeks later, I flew to Memphis for the weekend.

After I was home for a few hours, I asked my father to go out for a drive to discuss some things.

"Dad, on my birthday, I told Felix it was my birthday, and he left the pit and made a phone call. Then his brother, Jay, and Howard Neiland left the pit, and another broker showed up. Kevin Hisakawa stayed to handle the deck and regular business, and I worked the Prudential desk, and I executed a thousand crosses through them, and I think it was laundry. I think this is what they have planned for me." "Well, son, Dan would not be involved in anything that would be harmful to him legally. He is too smart for that. He always has plenty of insulation! But I will check it out for you."

After a pleasant weekend in Memphis I flew back to Chicago.

A few days later my father called and said, "Dan told me that none of the clerks or brokers on the floor can get into trouble for any kind of crosses as long as it is done by open outcry. Don't worry about it! Billy, it's all part of the game [business]." That satisfied me.

Then Lenny Capello, Henry Bandoni's nephew, came to the pit. I spoon-fed him and took great care of him. All he did was steal—he made so much money in out trades, it was ridiculous. Then one day, LIT handed me a large New Bridge International paper order. I gave it to Lenny—you should have seen the look on his face after he was used to doing all of the one lots. He split it with Kevin, and they raped the shit out of it.

I loved working with Lenny and Kevin. I learned all the tricks of the trade. Felix only came in part of the time, but he was the master, dumb like a fox.

CHAPTER 13

The Change in National Power

President George H. W. Bush lost to the rising star, William Jefferson Clinton. This was largely due to Ross Perot and Bush's late start in campaigning. Ross Perot, a Texas billionaire, ran with no political party affiliation, got on the ballot in almost every state, and paid for prime-time infomercials to explain how he would run the government. He said he would run the country like a private business. By running his campaign, he took the country for the first time into a three-candidate choice.

Ross Perot split some of the conservative vote and left the country fed up with two wealthy Texans. This gave the former governor of Arkansas the edge. Therefore my idol, President George Bush, who overthrew communism along with President Reagan and paved the way for the free market global economy we enjoy today, lost to Bill Clinton.

Shortly after the inauguration of President Clinton in 1993, my life changed.

The Experiment came into full swing.

I became more paranoid about the world and people around me, specifically, my employer. Up until that time, I fully trusted all of my true friends and was fully aware of who I was working for and trusted them.

The receptors in my brain began to rapidly fire, and I had the feeling of being on hallucinogenic drugs without taking any. I had never experienced this before.

I had increased anxiety and stomach troubles. I could not walk under an El track without first clinching my teeth and then puking my guts out. This had never occurred before. The stale air in the subways once inside the city also made me ill. I began to take cabs to work. But I could not walk to Barry's place from my apartment or to Murphy's pub and many other places in Chicago without walking under an El track.

I began to have auditory hallucinations and had conversations with myself on a regular basis. This had not previously occurred.

I began to have strong homosexual thoughts. When I masturbated to *Hustler* magazine, I would turn to the layout of sex between a man and a woman and fixate on the man. My masturbation sessions would also have heightened pleasure as I did this. This had never happened before.

Within a month of Clinton taking office, the operators of the Experiment were fully operating the controls.

CHAPTER **14**

The SEC Complaint Letter about Beathan Trading

Someone wrote a letter of complaint to the SEC (Securities Exchange Commission) about Beathan Trading. I can only speculate who did this, a customer, the operators of the Experiment, the executive branch of government, or Matt Pagani with someone's help off the floor.

Beathan had lost about $40 million of cattle customers' money. (People only complain when you lose money; there are no complaints if you are in the black.)

This letter put Beathan Trading under an investigation by the SEC. The letter of complaint (which I have never read) basically said that Beathan lump-sum traded accounts or pooled money, like a fund in the cattle. The letter went on to say they were not licensed to fund trade. Beathan argued that they were using Omnibus accounts and it was legal. But the SEC said that they needed larger margin requirements and that they had illegally cornered the livestock market. There were no convictions, but Beathan had to pay extremely high fines and was required to have more money backing their positions and smaller long-term holdings in the livestock market. My father personally had to pay a fifty-thousand-dollar fine. I got all this information secondhand from my father.

I do not honestly believe Matt was involved, but this was the first time the operators of the Experiment used my oral voice (auditory hallucinations).

A long time after the letter was written, I called my father, and the (oral voice) said, "Dad, you know that Matt, my old room-mate, might have written that letter to SEC. Did you know I had to move out of that place because he was dealing drugs? He had to have help because he is too stupid to have done it alone." My father inquired, "Who's this guy?"

The following evening, Matt called me on the phone and said, "Why did you call your dad and say all those bad things about me?" I replied, "What the hell are you talking about, and who told you that I called my dad and said bad things about you?" Matt countered, "You know you did!" "I do not know what the hell you're talking about." The conversation ended.

This interference by the operators of the Experiment led me to believe they were involved.

About a week later, Matt invited me over to his place. Matt buzzed me into the apartment from the street. I opened the inner door to the apartment, and Matt was sitting in the front room on a chair facing the door. He had on a T-shirt and sweatpants, as soon as I stepped in, he whipped his stiff, erect dick out of his sweatpants and smiled. I gave him a strange look and turned around and exited the apartment. He yelled after me, "Bill, come back. Let's go to a strip joint." I left the apartment and walked home.

Matt had a smoking-hot girlfriend named Gabriella, and I knew that they fucked regularly, but was Matt bisexual?

Was it possible someone told him to try to have sex with me? Were people slowly finding out about the Experiment? Who knew first and when?

CHAPTER 15

The Negotiation for My Seat

One morning in early January of 1993, Sidney walked onto the floor with a fresh IOM membership (seat) on his chest. I was envious.

The follow morning at breakfast with Dan, I asked, "Dan how long do you think it will take for International Futures and Options to give me a seat?" "Do you want to fill paper for them?" Dan inquired. "Yes, I do," I said. "Do you know what you're getting into?" "Yes." "Well, Billy, you won't have to stay with them forever, and all you have to do is ask." "Really?" Then, with a big grin, Dan said, "Yes, you'll get one hell of an education, and they really need some fresh blood—you're perfect!"

So the following morning I asked Felix if I could fill paper for International. Felix said, "Bill, you could end up like Donnie." I said, "I know that." Felix then said, "Well, let me go upstairs and find out exactly what you need."

Donnie was an indentured servant who had made a large

error and was paying for it one day at a time with half of his brokerage money. He might have been set up for this error because his brother was in prison, having been stung by the Feds (Dolphin Trading, the sting organization that framed brokers on the floor) years before I arrived. ABS may have set up poor old Donnie because they wanted to control him, or he made the error on his own. I honestly do not know which.

The next morning Felix sent me up to Henry Bandoni's office. I stopped at Henry's secretary's desk and said, "I understand Henry wants to speak with me." Standing at his office door, Henry said, "Yes, Bill, come in." We went in and sat down. Henry said, "I understand you want to fill paper for us. That's outstanding. You're a talented clerk. But if you leave us, we would expect to be paid back for our investment. Do we have an understanding?" "Yes, that seems more than fair, Henry," I eagerly replied. "The most cost-effective way to do this is to put you in an IOM seat for a year and have you continue to be a clerk, and then after a year, we will put you in a full seat to fill paper. Is that satisfactory?" "Yes, can I trade the markets while I clerk?" "Yes, we have allowed other brokers to do this in the past. Get ten thousand dollars, and we will set it up. I'll get you in next week's broker class, and you can take the exchange test right away." We stood up and shook hands.

I rode the elevator back to the trading floor on cloud nine again.

When I returned to the pit, Felix winked at me.

The next week I went through an intensive brokerage training class, took the test, and scored an 86 percent.

I asked Felix what acronym I should use on my seat; he replied, "BN", but when I went to compliance, this was already taken by another broker. So I came up with FWII, from my name, Francis William Nicholson II.

Then came the hard part. I asked my father for ten thousand dollars. He said, "I have not got it. You tell Henry to put up the money." I knew better than to ask Henry or Dan for money and thought about asking my rich uncle for the money, but this would have been an embarrassment to my father, and he might have even cut me off financially. So I elected not to trade my own account.

The next time I called Dan to thank him for the seat, the first thing he said was "It's worse than I thought, huh, Billy," referring to my father's financial condition.

Shortly after receiving my seat, one evening at home I typed up a proposed brokerage deal on my home computer and printed it out. It basically stated that all my brokerage income would be split fifty-fifty with International and I was responsible for my own errors.

I gave it to Felix the next morning in the pit. He read it and said, "It will be real close to this," and put it in his inside coat pocket to take up to Henry.

The next time I had breakfast with Dan, I asked, "If I have

a big error, can you take care of it?" He responded, "Billy, do you realize that International brokers have a job the next day if they have a large error, rather than being fired by their employers, which most brokerage groups do?" I pressed him further. Finally he said, "OK, I will take care of it, but you will never be able to work in the industry again."

This was putting a lot of pressure on Dan, but it was necessary because I had no money. Everything was in place after this breakfast, and I was excited about my future.

Then Henry took me to breakfast a few days later. We went across the street from the Merc to a popular spot for brokers. He was showing me off. At breakfast he informed me that I was in the most dangerous clerk position, and he wanted to move me to the cattle second option with his brother, Neil, to clerk there. I would have gotten an excellent education on deck handling and spreads.

But when I informed my father that I was moving to the cattle, he responded, "Not right now." Again, Max Beathan was a thorn in my side.

I went upstairs to Henry's office the next morning and informed him my father said I could not work in the cattle. He was furious and said, "I do not give a damn about Max Beathan. All I care about is you and Dan O'Connor, and Dan is your trump card. You need to hold it in your hand until you need it!!!"

I stayed in the Dmark, and this created a small rift with Henry.

CHAPTER **16**

The Beginning of Strange Behavior

On Thursday night, Matt called me and invited me over for pizza at Barry's and his place. He said, "Bring the bong." I did not bring the bong and walked over. When I arrived, Gabriella (Matt's girlfriend), Barry, and Matt were there. Barry asked to hang my coat up. The voice inside my head said, "Kid, Barry is trying to plant drugs in your coat."

They offered me some pizza, and Gabriella said, "I don't want any," with a strange look. I had a slice and instantly started hallucinating. This happened much too fast to have been caused by any hallucinogenic drugs in the pizza. The operators of the Experiment were at the controls causing this reaction in my brain and piped into my head, "Kid, the pizza is laced with AIDS." Then Matt said, "Don't worry, Bill—we will take care of you. We are your friends!"

Then at the end of the evening, Matt asked to share a cab to work the next morning. We had never shared a cab before. But I said, "OK, see you in the morning," and walked home, tripping hard.

In the morning, I hailed a cab in front of my apartment and told him to drive to 3828 North Sheffield, and then were headed to the Merc. We stopped out in front of Matt's place, and he appeared in the doorway with a large hockey bag weighing heavy off of his shoulder. As he got into the cab, I said, "What's in the bag?" He said, "Nothing." We pulled out for the Merc, and the cabbie blasted the radio. Immediately I knew something was up! I told the cabbie to turn down the radio and felt the outside of the bag. I felt a large, hard rectangular object that I assumed was a tape recorder. I stopped talking.

Matt opened his mouth halfway to the Merc and said, "Bill, why don't you move to Memphis and be a position trader? That's what you always talk about. That is what you want to do." I replied, "I have too much to learn right here at the Merc, and I want to work on the floor as a young man! What's up, Matt? Going to Memphis is not what I want to do."

We arrived at the Merc, and naturally Matt had no money, and I had to pay for the cab ride. As we got out of the cab, Matt said, "Well, you made it through the toughest part of the day." I remember thinking this was a very strange comment and conversation. I was also sure the bag was full of drugs.

I walked onto the floor, and everyone seemed to be looking at me. The operators of the Experiment were piping in extreme paranoia.

I walked to the Dmark pit. The bell rang, and the day began. The operator of the Experiment piped into my head, "They got your grandmother fired from Macy's." As the International's floor manager, Sam Gilman, walked by, the oral voice made me say, "Sam, never go near my grandmother again!" He looked at me in disbelief, and Jay turned around and said, "What?" I went back to watching my desks.

Then my break time came, and I went to the off-floor broker's bathroom, sat down, and started to shit. The oral voice kept repeating over and over, "I'm not going to break down today; hang tough." I'm sure I was overheard by more than one broker.

I went back to the pit, and the operators of the Experiment had me stare at Bill from Morgan Stanley. We had on the same shoes, oxblood bucks. When I was not getting orders from my desk, they had me stare at Bill and ran homosexual thoughts about him through my head. They kept saying, "Bill squared," inside my head, and continued with the homosexual thoughts. Bill was a former REFCO employee who hated Treston Lakeman.

The bell rang, and I had made it through the day. All my brokers gave me strange looks as I left the pit. I dropped off my coat at the broker's closet and caught a cab home as quickly as possible.

CHAPTER 17

The Weekend Prior to Charter

I arrived home from the exchange at 2:30 p.m. and immediately got high to take the edge off this stressful day. The operators of the Experiment were working overtime, piping all kinds of thoughts through my mind and having me say all kinds of disturbing things out loud.

About an hour later, I went to my bedroom, stripped naked and put my oxblood bucks back on my feet, crawled on top of my bed, and masturbated to homosexual thoughts of Bill from Morgan Stanley. The voice said out loud over and over, "Bill squared, you know you want him," and ran images through my head of me blowing him on the floor in front of everyone. I blew a huge load after jerking off hard for about an hour. I lay in bed in a pool of sweat with sperm all over my body for about another half hour, bewildered, and the voice kept saying aloud, "You know you enjoyed that!"

After that, I took my shoes off and took a hot shower for an hour and masturbated again in the shower. Then I cleaned up in the shower and turned the water to freezing cold for about ten minutes, turned off the water, and stepped out and put on my terry cloth robe.

I went over to the couch, sat down, and got high again. All kinds of strange thoughts were racing through my mind.

At this point, the shrinks would say this was a classic beginning to a manic episode, but the difference was that it was all piped in!

Then I ordered food in. I picked up the phone and ordered a tuna fish sandwich and clam chowder. I sat on the couch with my mind racing, and about forty-five minutes later, the food arrived. I ate half of the tuna sandwich first. Then took the lid off of the Styrofoam soup container, and stream rose off of the hot clam chowder. I began to consume the chowder when I came across a large ball of something—it oozed down the back of my throat. I immediately knew something was wrong and went to the bathroom toilet and threw up. The ball came back up my throat and splashed into the toilet surrounded by clam chowder. It looked like a large white spit ball. Then the operators of the Experiment said aloud, "It's sperm, kid, laced with AIDS."I took a second look, and that's what it looked like to me. Then the voice said inside my head, "You've got AIDS, kid; prepare for a slow death."

I went back and sat on the couch in my terry cloth robe with damp hair and freaked out a little and reached for the bong for relief.

After thirty minutes, I got up, brushed my teeth, and put on some street clothes for the weekend. My hair was dry by this point. I went back to the bathroom brushed it and put in some gel.

I sat back down on the couch again, while the operators of the Experiment piped in all kinds of crazy thoughts. Finally, my roommate Nathan walked in the door from work. Thank god, a reality check. He sat down on the couch next to me, and we had a conversation about what, I don't remember, but it was totally unrelated to the events of my day. He informed me that he had a gig that night—remember, he was a musician in a band. He did not get high with me. Later that night, he left for the gig.

About an hour after he left, the operators of the Experiment walked me into my bedroom and grabbed my copy of *Brokers, Bagmen, and Moles*. I had never read this book before. They started me on the introduction, which said right off the bat that the Feds "wanted to know more about Henry Bandoni and Charlton Templeton." My seat on the exchange (IOM membership) belonged to Charlton Templeton and was leased for me by Henry Bandoni (he put up the money). The operators of the Experiment said aloud, "You mean, it's true." Then they had me flip to the back of the book and look in the index and look up Justin Stoat (Donnie's brother). After I read a few passages about Justin, they shut the book, threw it aside, and again said out loud, "You mean, it's true."

Then the operators of the Experiment said aloud two or three times, "We can make you talk, kid." Remember, I was pretty stoned at this time, but I believe that the subconscious mind knew what was going on, but the conscious mind was still confused. My subconscious was quickly learning the tricks of the operators.

Then the operators of the Experiment said aloud, "Do you want to testify?"

I smoked pot the rest of the night and went to bed late.

I woke up around 3:00 p.m. the next day (Saturday).

I waked and baked (got high). Nathan, who was already up, did one bong hit with me. He smoked pot, but in small quantities. He asked me how I was doing, and I responded that I was having disturbing thoughts, but I was OK. He did not press me for information and said he was going over to his brother's apartment, which was in the neighborhood. As he was leaving, he asked, "Do you want to go out for a bite to eat tonight?" I said, "Sure." He then said, "I'll see you later then," and left.

I stayed in the apartment all day and smoked a lot of pot. The operators of the Experiment increased my paranoia of International by piping in a lot of strange thoughts.

Then Nathan returned in the evening, and we went to Murphy's for dinner. I had a Guinness and a brat with fries. Nathan asked, "What are the disturbing thoughts you're having?" The operators of the Experiment made me say aloud, "I believe I am working for the Mob, and they want to kill me!" Nathan looked shocked and said, "Do you think you're in danger of being shot or something?" The operators said, "YES!!!" Nathan reassured me and said, "I think you're OK, Bill." We finished dinner and walked home.

Nathan and I stayed up late and talked about the good old days at Sigma Chi at Wisconsin. Nathan's a good guy, and he knew how to take my mind off of things.

I slept in again on Sunday. I woke up and got high again. Nathan was not there.

Later, the phone rang, and it was Matt. He said, "You better stay away from the windows!" What a jerk!!! The operators took this ball and ran with it, piping in all the paranoia again.

The operators said aloud, "Whose team are you on? The Feds' or International's?"

Nathan came home late and said, "I'm beat. I'm going to bed," and went to his room.

I stayed up till 5:00 a.m. smoking pot and listening to the voice in my head and then went to bed.

CHAPTER **18**

The Morning before Charter

I overslept for work and woke up shaky and pale around 8:30 a.m. And Nathan was gone.

I immediately received a phone call from my father, and he said, "Dan called me, and you did not show up to work this morning and asked if you were on drugs. Everyone is very concerned about you. What's wrong?" "I don't know, Dad. Something is." "Can you make it in to work?" "I don't think I should." "Stay at home," and he hung up.

Then Sam Gilman called and said, "Where are you, and don't give me any bullshit." "I'm sick, and I'm going to stay home today!" Sam responded, "OK, we will see you tomorrow."

Then my dad called back and said, "Who were you talking to? The line was busy when I tried the first time." "Sam Gilman." "Who's that?" "Floor manager for International, and I told him I was sick and not coming in today." "What's wrong?" Then the operators of the Experiment said in my spoken voice over the phone to my father, "I think Henry Bandoni is going to try to kill me again." "Billy, no one is trying to kill you. You sit tight—I am going to get you home!"

I went into the bathroom and brushed my teeth, and the voice inside my head said, "The toothpaste is laced with cocaine." I got a numb feeling in my mouth, and my head began to feel like I was on cocaine. The operators of the Experiment were rapid-firing my neurons.

My father called back and said, "Billy, calm down. You're perfectly safe. I have an airline ticket for you at the airport for a 3:00 p.m. flight on United. It's a will-call ticket at the check-in desk. Can you do this?" "Yes." "Good." And then he hung up.

The operators of the Experiment then said inside my head, "Your apartment is bugged." Then they took me over to the bong and had me draw air through it with no flame or pot.

My mother then called, and I said, "It might have sounded like I got high, but I really did not." Then my mother said, "How much pot are you smoking?" "Not that much." "You need to pack a bag. Do you know what this means?" "Yes." "I love you, Billy. I'll see you tonight." And she hung up.

Then I called Dan on his private line and said, "Can I come see you?" He replied, "If you want, Billy." And I hung up.

The operators of the Experiment were obviously working overtime. And they said aloud in my spoken voice, "THE'RE GOING TO HIT YOU, KID!!!" I'm sure they were trying to make me believe that someone was going to kill me, but I took it to believe I was going to get arrested.

So I flushed all my pot and the baggy down the toilet. It was a lousy toilet, and not everything would flush, so I went to the kitchen, got a beer pitcher, filled it with water, took the lid off the back of the toilet, held the handle down, and poured the water in the back of the toilet. It worked. I obviously had done this before. Then I took my customer phone list from LIT and other paper documents from the exchange, burned them, and flushed them as well.

Almost done, I took the glass bong apart and put it in the dish washer, holding it in place with baggy ties, and put the small parts in the silverware basket. I started the dishwasher with soap.

Then I packed my hanging bag.

I blasted every radio in the house, including Nathan's stereo.

The operators of the Experiment then sent the hallucination of Henry Bandoni and Charlton Templeton being arrested at the exchange through my mind.

About an hour later, Nathan came home for lunch. He startled me when he walked in the door. He asked, "What are you do-ing?" He turned down the stereo and complained that I was blasting his brother's JBL speakers too loud. I told him, "I think the apartment is bugged, and I am going home to Memphis this afternoon." He said, "Good. You need to go home!" He left the apartment.

I hung out at home until 12:30 p.m. Then I dressed in khaki pants, a dress shirt, a tie, and my black leather coat. I walked out of the apartment and let a cab go by me on the street and then hailed him when he was a block past me. He backed up, and I got in and said, "Go to the airport."

As we pulled out onto the highway, the voice inside my head said, "You've got a tail." So I said to the driver, "Is there another way to the airport? In fact, drop me at the train." Then I took all of my IDs and credit cards and dropped them on the floor of the cab, except my Memphis, Tennessee, ID and cash, which I kept in my wallet. We arrived at the train. I paid the cabbie, got out, and walked up the stairs to the platform with my hanging bag in hand.

The train arrived, and I boarded and sat down. A man with a trench coat and brown leather accordion briefcase sat down across from me. The voice said in my head, "He's a hit man, kid." So I kept a close eye on the man and became sweaty with nervousness. I pulled off my tie and unbuttoned my shirt. Then I dropped the tie on the floor of the train, and the guy sitting behind me picked it up. The voice inside my head said, "That's a signal."

We arrived at the airport. I went up to the United ticket counter, showed my Memphis ID, and said, "I believe you have a will-call ticket for me to Memphis. My father set it up." The agent said, "Yes, Mr. Nicholson, just sign here." I signed, and as I was walking away from the counter, the voice said out loud in my spoken voice, "WHEN ARE THEY GOING TO HIT YOU, KID?"

Alarmed, I went into the bathroom, went into a stall, and opened my hanging bag. I took everything identifiable out of my bag: shirts and pants with my name written on them from the dry cleaners and my monogramed belt. I left only underwear and a few T-shirts and zipped the bag closed.

I walked to the gate. I had about an hour to wait before boarding, so I bought a hot dog and Coke from the stand, and the vender gave me change. It occurred to me that if I was going to get arrested, it would be upon departure in the plane from Memphis, because I had made it this far with no trouble. So I threw all my money out in an ashtray, leaving myself with only my Memphis ID.

I boarded the plane.

CHAPTER 19

The Plane

I boarded the plane, and I was seated in the coach-class cabin bulkhead, so the stewardess hung my hanging bag in the first-class closet. I sat down in my seat, and a man placed a brown leather accordion briefcase identical to the one that was on the train in the seat next to me. The stewardess said to me, "Is that your briefcase?" I said, somewhat alarmed, "no"; she took it out of the seat and put it in the overhead bin.

After the emergency introduction was over, the stewardess closed the first-class curtain, and I could no longer see the closet with my hanging bag.

Then the stewardess in the coach cabin started serving peanuts and soft drinks; like I said, I was in the bulkhead, so I was served first. I ordered a Coke, as soon as I downed the Coke, I felt like I was on cocaine again.

After twenty minutes, I went to the bathroom and took a monster shit, and the voice kept saying aloud, "They planted it in your bag, kid." I spent about fifteen minutes in the head and returned to my seat.

Then the stewardess in first class opened the curtain, and a man two seats in front of me across the aisle was looking at eight-by-ten glossy photographs of Beechcraft aircrafts. He was holding then in the aisle and shuffling through them.

We started down on our final descent, and I began to recite out loud to myself, "I'm a student, and I live at 3953 Minden Road, Memphis, Tennessee, 38111," over and over again as I stared at my ID.

We landed and taxied to the gate. People started to deplane, and I stood up, walked past the first-class hanging closet, and left the plane without my bag. As I walked up the sky ramp, I prepared to get arrested. I reached the door to the airport, and no one was there. I started to walk down the hallway, when I was met by my parents. My mother asked, "Did you bring any luggage?" I responded, "No."

We walked to the car.

I got in the car, and the operators of the Experiment said inside my head, "Your parents are wired, kid." So I said very little in the car. We arrived at home.

CHAPTER 20

The Breakdown at Home

We walked into the house. My mother asked to hang up my jacket. I would not surrender it to her. I said, "I want to hang onto to it. I sat down on the floor in the middle of the living room. I took my jacket off and set it beside me.

My parents warmed up dinner for me in the microwave. I refused to eat it.

I then said, "I think I am under some kind of an investigation." My father, with a beet-red face and with his voice three octaves higher than usual, pointed his almighty finger of authority at me and yelled, "YOU ARE NOT IMPORTANT ENOUGH TO BE UNDER ANY KIND OF INVESTIGATION!!!"

My mother gave me a sealed bottle of water. I cracked the cap and drank. Again the operators rapid-fired my neurons, and I felt like I was on cocaine.

I got up off the floor, grabbed my coat, ran out of the house, and said, "Even my own parents!" I ran down the driveway and into the street. I ran hard for three blocks and stopped. I was standing in the middle of an intersection in the neighborhood. It was a cold, misty, rainy night. I realized I had no money and nowhere to go. I slowly walked back to the house. As I reached the yard of my parents' house, a car came rushing up on me. I ran into the bushes. Then I recognized the driver, my father. I walked back into the house. My father was coming in through the garage door. I said, "You scared the shit out of me." He responded, "Well, you're scaring the shit out of me too."

I began to cry and said in hysteria, "I'm not a drug dealer. Dad, do you know any reason why I should have AIDS?" He replied, "No! Why? Is there a reason you may have been exposed to AIDS?" "NO." "You do not have AIDS!"

The operators of the Experiment made me say aloud, "Are the Doolans (my cousins) dead?" My parents looked at each other in disbelief.

I said, "Do you know any reason why anyone is trying to kill me?" My father quickly said, "NO ONE IS TRYING TO KILL YOU!!!"

The phone rang. My father answered it and said, "Max, who has the best drug rehab in town? OK, where is Charter located?" He wrote down the directions and the address and hung up the phone.

"We are going to Charter Lakeside Hospital for drug rehab." I asked, "Are we going for drug rehab or protection?" He said, "BOTH."

We got in the car and drove to Charter.

On the way, my mother asked, "Did you pack a bag?"

"FUCK THE BAG!!"

My father took a wrong turn pulling into Charter and drove down a dark alley. I said, "Turn around. You're scaring me."

We arrived at Charter.

Were the operators of the Experiment getting ready to kill me and blame it on Henry to tidy up the mess? I do not think so, but it was a possibility. I was really scared at this point!!

Also, Max Beathan was back at the helm—he chose the hospital!!

CHAPTER **21**

Charter Lakeside Hospital

We walked from the car through the double doors at Charter and sat down in the lobby. My father kept saying, "HENRY BANDONI MUST HAVE SET THIS UP. THIS MUST HAVE COST A FORTUNE." The receptionist gave us forms to fill out, including ones on insurance provider and the living will. The living-will question freaked me out, and I said, "I want to live as long as possible. Never pull the plug!"

Then the nurse appeared to take me to drug rehab. I hugged my mother and turned to my father and said, "There is something to all of this, Dad." My parents exited the hospital, and the nurse took me through a doorway and down the hallway. We arrived at a security door, and she used her badge to open it.

The first thing she had me do was stop at a bathroom and piss in a cup. Then she sat me down in front of the nurses' station.

From there she took me into a small room and asked, "What brought you to the hospital?" I asked, "Is this being recorded?"

She said, "No." I then said, "I wish it was." She responded, "You wish it was?" I said, "Yes." "Well, it is not, and now tell me what brought you to the hospital?" I opened up and said, "I believe someone is trying to kill me, maybe my employer, and I might be under some kind of an investigation." She then stood up and said, "We'll talk further in the morning. Let's go to your room."

We walked to the room. She took me into the room and said, "Your bed is the one nearest the window." I said, "Am I safe here?" She said, "Yes." I sat down on my bed in the dark. After a few minutes, I stood up and stared out the window. There was a light misty rain coming down; the only view was a field of dead grass in front of a chain-link fence and a forest of trees with no leaves behind that.

Then the operators of the Experiment said over and over inside my head, "We killed your parents, kid." After listening to this for about twenty minutes, I believed it. So I left the room and went to the nurses' station and asked to use the phone. They said, "We do not allow outgoing calls at this time of night; the phones are turned off." I turned around and there were wall phones and one pay phone. I had an AT&T calling card memorized, so I picked up the pay phone, dialed my parents, 0 (901) 680-0711, and plugged in my calling card number. My mother answered, half-asleep, and said, "Hello." The voice inside my head said, "It is not her, kid; they are dead." So I said, "Mom." "Yes." "What was the name of our Irish setter?" "Hillary and, Billy, you woke me up. I am going back to sleep now." She hung up. I believed they were alive. Our Irish setter had been dead for ten years; only she or my father would know the proper answer.

Then I turned around to the nurses' station and said, "I know you have my room bugged."

I went back into my room and sat back on my bed, and the voice in my head said, "You've got AIDS, kid. You're dead anyway," and flooded me with homosexual thoughts. My dick got hard for about an hour, but my roommate was in the bathroom using the light to write in his journal, so there was no place to jack off, so I sat there in agony, and finally my dick went limp.

I did not sleep at all that night, and my head was racing with all kinds of crazy thoughts.

In the wee hours of the morning, I got off my bed and went to the nurses' station and asked to get a drink of water. A very nice nurse took me over to the sink opposite the nurses' station and grabbed a cup and filled it with water. I said, "Is it OK to drink?" She placed the cup to her lips and took a sip and grabbed me another cup and handed it to me. I reached for the cup that she had drunk from and used it to drink three full glasses of water. Then she said, "Why don't you try to get some sleep?"

I went back in my room sat down on my bed and stared out the window; the rain had stopped. I watched the sun come up.

Then a nurse with needles and vials entered my room. I hate needles. I stared out the window as she prepared a needle and vial. I turned around and saw the needle and freaked out a little. She saw my face and said, "Wait. You did not see me do that!" and pulled a fresh sealed needle and prepared the syringe again. I said, "Thanks, and can you take enough blood for an AIDS test too?" She said, "Sure, if that's what you want." She drew a lot of blood and left.

After that, another nurse came into my room and said, "Time for breakfast." I went out to the dining room but did not eat anything.

Then a doctor came in and gave me a physical. When he was finished, he asked, "Why did you ask for an AIDS test?" What could I say? He was not going to buy pizza laced with AIDS or sperm soup. So I thought for a moment and remembered Jamaica. I had taken a vacation to Jamaica and picked up a prostitute and had a tough time getting it up, so she played with my dick and bit me on the chest a few times. I did have a condom on and never got my rocks of with her, just paid her and left. The next night of that vacation I picked up a local girl in a bar, took her back to the hotel, and fucked her twice that night and once in the morning, all with condoms. So I told the doctor, "I picked up a prostitute in Jamaica, and she bit me in the chest a few times!"

Now I got a social worker with all the standard questions. "Have you ever been sexually abused?" "No." "Have you ever been physically abused?" "No." "Have you ever been verbally abused?" "A little bit by my father." And so on.

I called my mother and said, "They gave me a AIDS test. I'm worried about the old switcheroo. Please come to the hospital." "I can't, Billy; I have an appointment with a client." "If you love me, you'll come." "OK."

Then I called my father at work and said, "Dad, I told them that you never sexually abused me but that you verbally abused me." He hung up the phone.

After that, they gave me a shrink. He kept saying, "Calm down, Bill. You are perfectly safe here."

We were standing at the nurses' station when my mother arrived. I broke down into hysteria, crying, unable to complete entire thoughts or sentences, using fragmented, pressured speech. I was pale, shaky, and nervous as I fell to the floor. The doctor then told my mother, "This is not a drug problem; it is a psychological one. I am going to place Bill in the care of Dr. Paxton in the psychiatric ward here at the hospital." I stood up and collapsed into my mother's arms, still crying. This was a total breakdown. The operators of the Experiment had completed a total brainwash and pushed my mind over into psychosis.

My mother stood there holding me in disbelief.

The three of us walked over to the ward, and the doctor introduced me to Chris, a psych tech. I asked the doctor, "Is this guy OK?" "Yes, he is safe!"

I told my mother that I loved her and I was sorry!!! She told me that she loved me too!!! Then the doctor told her it would be best if the two of them left me with Chris, and they walked away talking.

I sat down at a small table with Chris.

Chris showed genuine concern for me.

I tried to talk to him, but I was bouncing from topic to topic in fragmented speech.

I discussed flying, friends, the exchange, Chicago, and drugs.

Then I noticed we were wearing the same shoes, oxblood bucks. The operators of the Experiment started in on the homosexual fixation. Those shoes: Bill from Morgan Stanley, Chris the tech, and I were all wearing the same shoes. A strange coincidence. The operators of the Experiment sent thoughts through my mind of Chris and me having sex. Chris was also wearing a necklace. The operators asked in my spoken voice, "Where did you get that beautiful necklace?" Chris smiled and said, "A friend."

At this point the operators were in total control and started me flirting with Chris. This fixation and flirtation did lead to a little trust, and I calmed down enough to speak.

I told Chris that I thought my former roommates slipped me a mickey in a slice of pizza and I began to trip after eating it. I also said that my walk home after eating it was very difficult because I tripped hard.

He asked, "Have you ever felt this way before?" I replied, "Yes, when I did acid." He then said, "I am going to step away for a moment. Will you be OK?" "Yes."

This was all the ammunition the shrinks needed to begin a Haldol regimen. What a mistake it had been to bring up acid.

Then Chris returned, followed by a nurse with a small cup in her hand. Chris asked me, "Bill, will you drink this?" I asked, "What is it?" "Orange juice." I drank the substance and asked, "What else was in it?" The nurse said, "Something to help you organize your thoughts." What a bunch of bullshit that was. The substance was Haldol, and it made me more susceptible to the Experiment operators' control.

My vision blurred, and my speech became garbled, so they gave me more, without orange juice this time. I was the most drugged I had ever been in my life. The operators in my spoken voice started to tell Chris I worked for the Mob and they were trying to kill me. I tried to stop speaking but with little success. So they gave me more Haldol. At this point, I had a ton of liquid Haldol in my system.

I stood up from the small table and paced the small hallway. Then Chris suggested that I go sit down in the dayroom just off the hallway. So I walked in and sat down in a recliner. The room was a small box with a closed window on one side that the nurses could watch through from the back of a nurses' station.

There was one other patient in the room. He asked Chris for a cigarette and asked me if I wanted one. I said, "Sure, thanks!" Chris gave us each a cigarette, and the other patient sat down next to me, and Chris lit our smokes. What a relief the nicotine and smoke in my lungs were.

I sat in the recliner for about twenty minutes and then got up, went back out in the hallway, and began pacing, again. I was really confused at this point.

Then the nurse came back up to me with another cup of Haldol. I said, "I think I have had enough of that shit!!!" She responded, "If you don't drink it, we will give you a shot in the ass!!!" I said, "OK, but that is it!!!" and drank it. She asked me to sit down with Chris at the small table again. So I did. Then she asked, "Do you believe your body is full of bugs?" The operators of the Experiment ran a mental image through my mind of insects inside my body. So I said, "NO."

Reflecting back, this question makes me believe that the shrinks at Charter had knowledge of the Experiment. I also found out after I left the hospital that this nurse was the wife of Dr. Paxton, the attending shrink.

Then the other patient and I were served dinner at a small table in the dayroom. We were provided Styrofoam containers with plastic spoons to eat with. I did manage finally to eat something.

Then the shift change came, and Chris traded places with a cute young black girl. We sat at the small table in the hallway, and I was a natural flirt with her!

After about an hour of my chatting and flirting with her, she was called away. After about ten minutes, she reappeared through the double security doors with a large, square, blue suitcase. She set it down on the floor in front of me and unzipped it. Inside were brand-new clothes, and she said, "It looks like someone went shopping for you!" I replied, "My mother is wonderful!!" and went into the bathroom and changed clothes.

The Haldol was finally setting in and shutting down some of my receptors. I began to calm down and continued to talk and flirt with the young black girl.

I was still very hyped up, or manic, if that's what you want to call it, so the desire to seduce was very high. Let's say I was very horny.

Around ten o'clock, the young black girl said, "Why don't you try to get some sleep." Remember, I had not slept for about forty-eight hours. The bedroom or dorm was on the opposite side of the hall from the dayroom, a small room with about ten single-level beds. My bed was the one closest to the door to the hallway. The other patient in the ward was already asleep in a bed on the far side of the room.

I lay down and tried to sleep and tossed and turned for about two hours. Then a large black female nurse came in the room with a cup of water and a huge pill. I said, "What is that? Do I have to take it?" She kindly said, "Yes, if you want to sleep and recover so you can reenter mainstream society with all your friends!" I took the pill and was asleep thirty minutes later.

I was awakened by another psych tech, a beautiful blond-haired, blue-eyed young woman also named Kris.

She walked me into the dayroom, and I ate breakfast.

After breakfast, I sat down at the small table in the hallway with Kris and tried to flirt. She played the bitch; either she was hot and knew it and this was natural, or this was by design. I'm not sure which.

Slowly she warmed up to me. And asked how I slept. Then I got a large glass of Haldol.

A large man, who looked to be in his fifties, walked into the hallway. Kris said, "This is your doctor, Bill. His name is Dr. Paxton." I stood up and shook his hand. Then he took me off of the hallway to a small room.

He began by saying, "I understand you believe someone is trying to kill you, and you previously worked for the Mob. Tell me about this." The operators of the Experiment opened my mouth and said so much I could not keep up because of all the Haldol I was on. What a setup.

Finally Dr. Paxton said, "I think you've said enough. Will you work with me on your problems?" I said, "I guess." "There is a psychologist I trust. Will you be willing to speak with her as well?" asked Dr. Paxton. I said, "OK." "I enjoyed talking with you, Bill. Let's go back to the ward." We walked back to the small hallway.

I sat down with Kris, and we chatted for about an hour, and then I said, "I think I am going to take a nap. I have a hangover from the sleeping pill and all the Haldol." She said, "That sounds like a good idea."

Shortly after I got to sleep, I was awaked by the psychologist.

She asked me some background questions, and she began to play with her strand of pearls. Then she asked, "What is your sexual preference?" I answered, "Heterosexuality. But lately I have been having some homosexual thoughts." She said, "Tell me about these homosexual thoughts." Again the operators of the Experiment took over my speech, and I was along for the ride. They spoke a little slower this time, and what I remembered them saying, which was true, was that I had not tried homosexual sex, yet!

This doctor dwelled on the homosexuality and asked me nothing about the stress of my job, the employers I was working for, or the belief that my life was in danger. This pretty much sealed the door on the setup.

She reiterated, "So you have been having homosexual thoughts for about two months, and they plague you throughout the day, right?" What could I say? "I guess."

I hung out with Kris the rest of the day and flirted with her.

After dinner, the shift change came, and the cute young black girl came back.

I sat at the small table with her for about and an hour; then she stood up and said, "Come over here—there is something I want to tell you." We walked over near the security doors, and she said, "We got the results back from your blood tests, and you do not have AIDS." "Are you sure?" I questioned. Reassuringly she said, "We're sure you definitely don't have AIDS." I said, "That is a relief."

Interesting that they had the black girl tell me, huh?

Around ten o'clock, I went to bed. The male Chris woke me up. After breakfast I sat down at the small table in the hallway and there were clay figures on the table: a huge blue dick and a red half bust of a man with his mouth wide open and large blue lips. Chris asked with a smile, "Are you a homosexual?" I said, "I do not think so." He continued smiling at me, and I got a raging hard dick. The operators of the Experiment flooded me with homosexual thoughts. Finally I rolled my eyes at Chris, got up, went to the bathroom, and pulled down my pants. I sat down on the toilet and began to stroke my hard dick. I looked up, and through the ventilation duct, I saw a red light. I realized I was on video. But I did not stop. I stroked harder and blew a load all over the toilet seat. I sat there for a while with my back leaning against the back of the toilet, totally relaxed. Finally, I used toilet paper to clean up the mess, pulled up my pants, zipped and buttoned my fly, and walked out of the bathroom, embarrassed. I did not go back into the hallway. I sat down on my bed, bewildered, again. From that day forward, every shrink I have been to accuses me of being a homosexual.

They left the clay figures on the table for two more days and left a tube sock in my bed for me to jack off into. I did jack off in bed the next night to homosexual thoughts and blew a load into the sock.

On the third day, they rolled the clay figures into a ball of red and blue clay and left it on the table. I guess this is Southern-style homosexual treatment. I never jacked off at the hospital again—jack off twice, and you're a fag.

On the forth day, they allowed my mother to come visit me, and she asked if it would be OK if my father came to visit me on the fifth night. I said, "Sure."

On the morning of the fifth day, they gave me a journal and told me I should start writing in it and to write my name on the cover. I said, "I will write both my names on it," and wrote, "Bill Nicholson" and "Francis William Nicholson II" on the cover. They made a big deal out of this. Schizophrenia.

The operators of the Experiment wrote in the journal with my hand. They called all my fraternity brothers at Sigma Chi at Wisconsin fags. Nothing could be further from the truth. I do not know of any fags in my fraternity. And then they had me give it to my father when he arrived that night. Pretty shitty, wouldn't you say!

The shrinks were expecting there to be some kind of trouble with my father and my meeting on the fifth night. It went off without a hitch, except for the journal, which he later read.

That evening I was with Kris, the female tech, sitting at the small table, when they brought in another patient. He was crying and very distraught. Kris told me that he had been homosexually raped. He went straight into the dorm with a small bag and went into the bathroom. I could hear the shower running a few minutes later. After about fifteen minutes, a loud ponding noise came from the bathroom; he was probably pounding on the walls of the shower. The nurses ran into the bathroom, and the noise stopped.

Kris said, "You should try to talk to him. You probably have a lot in common." What a bitch! I avoided him the rest of my stay.

In hindsight, what Kris had said was true. I did not realize at the time that I was being homosexually raped both mentally and physically by the operators of the Experiment and that my own inhibitions made me avoid this poor young man.

At the end of the week, they moved me off of the ward and gave me a roommate in a private room, in the less intensive psycho side of the hospital. Then for two weeks they sent me through drug and alcohol rehab classes, along with regular visits from Dr. Paxton and the psychologist.

I quickly came out of the psychosis after the move.

At the end of the first week, Kris, the cute blond, said, "You know, you have to ask Dr. Paxton to leave the hospital." I did. And they discharged me a week later.

I was discharged on the drugs Haldol and Cogentin (for side effects) with the diagnosis of paranoid delusional and as a homosexual.

I spent three horrible weeks at Charter Lakeside Hospital.

CHAPTER **22**

UT Medical

My parents were very displeased with the care I received at Charter Lakeside Hospital; therefore, they made an appointment with the University of Tennessee Medical.

Two days after my discharge from Charter, we went to UT Medical and met with a psychiatrist named Dr. Underhill.

The meeting took place with the doctor, my parents, and me.

Dr. Underhill asked me to describe the events that brought me to Charter. I said, "I thought someone was trying to kill me, maybe my employer, and I felt I was under some kind of an investigation." I went on to describe the strange behavior I exhibited prior to Charter.

Dr. Underhill then said, "You're not paranoid delusional. I can tell by looking at you that you are bipolar. The events and your beliefs are a classic bipolar episode."

He made this diagnosis after meeting with my parents and

me for fifteen minutes. This diagnosis would cause me to lose my pilot medical for the rest of my life, and I will never fly an airplane as pilot in command again in my life.

This is the diagnosis every future shrink would cling to, and later schizoaffective would be added. Therefore, my present diagnosis is bipolar schizoaffective.

Dr. Underhill said, "You should not be on Haldol but instead, Lithium," and gave me a drug regimen to go onto Lithium and slowly taper off of Haldol and Cogentin.

Then my father asked, "Is Billy OK to go back to work?" Quickly Dr. Underhill said, "Yes, work is good; it provides structure." Dr. Underhill had no knowledge of how stressful working on the exchange floor was and how difficult it would be to do my job on three psychotropic drugs.

He then said, "If you feel another episode coming on, get on an airplane."

Then my father said, "Billy was also concerned about having AIDS." I responded, "They gave me an AIDS test in the hospital, and I do not have it." Dr. Underhill said, "Sometimes the first test is not accurate; you might want to take another one." Disgusted with this doctor, I said, "I do not have AIDS."

Within an hour, I was presented with fresh script for Lithium and a regimen to taper off of Haldol and Cogentin. And marching orders to go back to work!

Dr. Underhill definitely did not do me any favors.

This left only the weekend for me to get used to the drugs and recover, because my father booked me on a Sunday night flight back to Chicago, to begin work Monday morning.

On Sunday morning, my father told me to tell everyone I was working for on the floor that I had been gone for a month for drug and alcohol rehabilitation for marijuana. He said, "Half the floor smokes the stuff, so this should put their minds at ease."

I boarded a plane for Chicago that night!

CHAPTER **23**

Returning to the Exchange

When I got back to my apartment, I was glad to see Nathan. I told him I was off of pot but doped up on psychotropic drugs, and I was not sure I could do my job. He said, "Just do your best and don't worry about it."

I went to sleep.

I woke up early in the morning with a hangover from all the drugs. I took a shower and dressed and caught a cab to the exchange.

When I arrived on the floor, everyone was glad to see me. Shortly after the market opened, Zach asked me, "Where have you been for a month?" I responded, "I was in drug rehab for a month for my addiction to marijuana." Then everyone said, "Who cares about marijuana?" So far, so good.

Everyone from the company kept bringing me paychecks from when I was gone, four in total.

The market was quiet all morning long, thank god. But then the afternoon came, and things picked up, and I had trouble keeping up with LIT and Lind Waldock. Then one of the arbitrage traders in the front row gave me a three-lot order. I gave it to Felix and watched him execute the trade right as the market rallied hard, and he put it in his top pocket and pulled out the deck from his lower pocket to chase the market. He did not give me a confirmation, and I was busy with my desks, so I told the arbitrage trader, "Nothing done." The trader was furious, and this was a mistake or error on my part.

About twenty minutes later, Felix handed me the three lot, and it was a huge winner. I asked the arbitrage trader if he wanted it, another mistake. He said, "Not now!!!"

All of my brokers were staring at me because I was nowhere near my par.

I gave the card to Felix and said, "It's a winner, but it's an error."

Felix then said, "Bill, why don't you take break and go talk to Henry?" It was about 12:45 p.m., and the market closed at 2:00 p.m.

I went to Henry's office and asked his secretary to speak with him. She sent me into his office. Henry said, "Sit down, Bill. What's wrong with you?" I replied, "They tell me I am bipolar." And I began to cry. "They have me on three drugs, and I don't think I can do my job!!!" Henry then opened the left-hand drawer of his desk and began writing down phone numbers. When he finished, he said, "Bill, the exchange will always be here, and when you're ready, you can come back! These are all my numbers. If you need anything in Chicago, you call me!!!!" Henry was very compassionate and showed genuine concern for me. It was ridiculous that the operators of the Experiment had tried to make me believe that he was trying to kill me.

Henry then said, "Go back down on the floor and tell everyone the truth and make it through the day. Then take as much time as you need, and remember, you can always come back and work for me!!!"

When I got back to Dmark pit, it was 1:15—only forty-five minutes to go.

Zach again asked, "Why was it you took time off?" I told the truth this time. "I was in a psychiatric hospital, and I'm bipolar and on psychotropic drugs." "Then why did you tell us you were in drug rehab?" "Because my father told me to tell everyone that."

The market got a little busy on the close, and it took all my ability to sort the cards for my two desks after the close. Felix went and talked to the arbitrage trader that I had hung. I finished by giving the last of my cards to Roy at the LIT desk, shook his hand, and left.

I immediately crawled in a cab and left. It had been a horribly difficult day.

CHAPTER **24**

Mother to the Rescue

I stepped out of the cab at my apartment and went inside. It was around 2:30 p.m. Shortly after I sat down on the couch, my mother called. "Billy, I am getting on a plane to Chicago in an hour. I will call you from the hotel when I arrive." I replied, "Great, Mother, I can really use your support. I love you, and I will see you soon!"

I sat on the couch totally depressed, wondering what I was going to do with my life at this point.

Nathan came home around 5:30. I recounted the events of the day and told him my mother was coming. He sat down on the couch next to me and tried to lift my spirits.

Around 8:00, my mother called and told me which hotel she was booked into downtown. I wasted no time: I crawled into a cab and was downtown by 9:00.

I walked into the hotel and picked up a house phone and asked for her room; they connected me. My mother picked up the phone and gave me her room number. I went up to the room, and I was in her arms crying in no time at all.

I told her, "Mother, there was no way I could do my job on all the drugs, and I did not have enough time to recover from my breakdown!" "I know, Billy. That is why I am here. It's OK."

I stopped crying, and we chatted about what to do next. We decided to fly back to Memphis the next afternoon.

I spent the night with her in her room on a rollaway bed. In the morning we ate breakfast and checked out. We caught a cab up to my place and packed a bag and then left for the airport. We were in Memphis by nightfall.

My father picked us up at the airport.

My father on the drive home was also very supportive, saying, "Billy, it is not the end of the world. We'll find something new for you to do!"

When we arrived home, my father grilled a steak dinner for us. We sat down to dinner, and my father asked, "Billy, what would you like to do next?" "Well, I would like to return to Chicago, take a break, and take a class for the series three [the off-floor brokerage test] and pass it, while all the commodities information is fresh in my head. And then relax for a while in order to find something to do outside the commodities business." My father said, "That sounds like an excellent plan."

As we were finishing dinner, my mother said, "We would like

to take you back to see Dr. Underhill while you're here—is that OK?" Believing that I was bipolar, I said, "Sure."

I went to bed upstairs in my parents' home.

I slept late and woke up and went downstairs. My mother greeted me and asked, "How did you sleep?" "Well." "We have an appointment with Dr. Underhill at 4:30 p.m. today." "OK, I'll take a shower."

I hung out with my mother, and my father came home early from work, around 3:45, and we headed down to UT Medical.

We walked into Dr. Underhill's office, and all sat down.

I started by saying, "I was unable to do my job because you had me on three psychotropic drugs, and I had not com-pletely recovered from my breakdown." Dr. Underhill said, "I am sorry. I did not realize how stressful and intense your job was." I remember thinking that it was a little late for an apology, but for some reason, my parents had confidence in this quack. I went on to say, "I do not know if it's a combina-tion of the three drugs, but I am having a hard time tolerating Lithium." Dr. Underhill said, "Do not worry about it. You'll get used to it." Another lie. I never tolerated Lithium well, even after I was off of Haldol and Cogentin.

We sat and listened to the rest of Dr. Underhill's bullshit and left.

When we arrived home, my father informed me that he was

thinking of buying a new Lexus and asked me, "Do you want my old 533i BMW?" I said, "Are you sure, Dad? That would be great!!"

The next day, my father bought a new Lexus and gave me the BMW.

My mother set up an appointment in Chicago with the head of the University of Chicago Medical psychiatric department for two weeks later. She accomplished this because Dr. Levison's daughter Beverly went to Harvard Law School with my sister, and Dr. Levison was the head of U of Chicago Medical.

At the end of the week, I drove back to Chicago.

CHAPTER **25**

Bumming around Chicago Depressed

I drove straight through to Chicago. It took me nine hours. I enjoyed driving my 1984 manual transmission 533i BMW.

When I arrived at my apartment, Nathan was asleep. I hung out for a few hours, listening to music, and then crashed.

I woke up early and called my parents and told them I had made it to Chicago and went back to bed.

Later I woke up, and Nathan was awake. I told him I was going to take the series three and find something new to do. His comment was "Maybe the exchange wasn't meant to be."

All of my friends were very supportive and tried to cheer me up that weekend.

On Monday morning I checked into a class for the series three, and it began that evening for two weeks. So I started attending.

On Thursday my mother flew in again, and we went to the psychiatrist at the University of Chicago on Friday afternoon. He was very nice and seemed to be the most intelligent shrink I had met so far. My mother was busy fixing me—she had spent the last week reading everything she could on the subject of bipolar. My mother detailed how I had been bipolar all my life. This was untrue and unhelpful. It was just like fixing dyslexia all over again. The doctor made an appointment with me for a week later, but alone this time.

Don't get me wrong—I appreciate my mother's concern, but she can get a little overzealous.

I spent the weekend with my mother. We ate at nice restaurants and went shopping on the Magnificent Mile. She flew home Sunday night.

The following Friday afternoon, I went back to the U of Chicago shrink. I walked into his office, sat down, and told him I was feeling better because I was finally off of Haldol and Cogentin. His first comment to me was "You look a lot better to me without your mama tagging along." This made me laugh. He then asked, "Do you think you're bipolar?" I responded, "I don't know. Everyone has been telling me I am." "Well, I would like to set you up with a psychiatrist in the city, Dr. Hightsman, and the two of you can sort it out. How's that sound?" "OK, I'll give it a try," I replied. He gave me Dr. Hightsman's phone number, and we shook hands, and I left.

That night I went and took the series three test and passed with a ninety-three.

On Monday morning I called Dr. Hightsman and set up an appointment for later that week.

I spent six more months in Chicago, bumming around and going to see Dr. Hightsman once a week.

During this time, at Nathan's suggestion, I smoked pot again.

Then my father called and said, "Billy, you need a change. You're stale in that town.—you need to move. How about Aspen?" "OK, I guess."

I began flying back and forth between Aspen and Chicago, to set up my life in Aspen.

CHAPTER 26

Setting Up My Life in Aspen

I flew into Aspen. Stephanie Wentworth picked me up at the airport. Stephanie is my favorite of my parents' friends and is a close personal friend of mine. She welcomed me into her home with great generosity.

She had a good friend, Jacqueline, who worked at Pitkin County Dry Goods, a clothing store, and Jacqueline arranged an interview for me with Jacob, the owner of the store. I landed a job there the first week.

This left the housing problem. I tried for a long time to find a place but with little success. Then I met Raymond Marrow. Raymond showed me a basement shoebox apartment that was a maintenance person's apartment for rental condos he had available. The entrance was through the garage parking, but the location was great, right at the base of Aspen Mountain and two blocks from work on Durant Street. So I took it.

I spent a few more very enjoyable days with Stephanie and flew back to Chicago.

When I got back to Chicago, Matt asked to go to Aspen with me. I had mixed emotions about Matt. Friend or foe? I felt like he had some key to the strange things that had happened to me in the last six months. And you know the old adage: keep your friends close and your enemies closer. So, I agreed.

It was really hard to leave my true friends, Nathan Baxter and Barry Martin.

Everyone helped load up the U-haul that Matt and I towed behind the BMW.

The next morning, Matt and I headed for Aspen. We made it all the way to Colorado without any problems. Then, on an elevated road after the Eisenhower Tunnel at night, I was face-to-face with a deer in the middle of the road. I clipped the poor deer with the left front headlight and grill, on the driver's side, and the deer swung around and hit the rear driver's side passenger door. We stopped and got out; the deer was nowhere to be found. The car was still running, and the headlight was pushed in but still lit. So, we continued to Aspen. The car was never the same after that!

We drove straight to the house of another fraternity brother of mine, Nick Milligan, who lived on Cemetery Lane in Aspen. Stephanie lived up on the side of a mountain, and there was no way of getting the car and U-haul up there. We pulled along the edge of the driveway and shut off the car. Then, just to see the damage that the deer had done, I tried the ignition again, and it did not turn over. We crashed at Milligan's place.

In the morning, Milligan gave Matt and me a ride up to Stephanie's place because Milligan's roommates did not want us crashing on the couch.

Two days later, when Milligan had spare time, we hooked the U-haul up to his Toyota pickup and moved me into my apartment and took the U-haul and trailer hitch down to the valley to turn it in. We came back, jumped the BMW, and drove it to the apartment garage of my apartment.

All in all, Matt turned out to be a good friend.

I was settled in Aspen and started work the following week.

CHAPTER **27**

Pitkin County Dry Goods

In the beginning, my employment with Pitkin County Dry Goods went well. Everyone was very supportive.

Then everyone started asking me, "Why are you here, Bill?" Day after day my coworkers would ask me this question suspiciously.

Then I got in a small spat with Amber when she asked me this question. I countered, "Why the hell do you live in Aspen? I've been coming here since childhood."

Obviously, the employees had knowledge of the Experiment.

Then Alec, the arrogant homosexual manager, called me into his office and asked me why Amber and I had had a misunderstanding. I replied, "Obviously she does not like me. I know she works on commission, and Jacob claims no one does. She and Jacob have a Jewish bond of faith, and she shines his balls." I had had enough of the bullshit from everyone. So that's what I told him.

I came to work the next day, Christmas Eve, and Alec canned me. I said, "I want to talk to Jacob." Alec replied, "He does not have time to speak with you." "You better tell him to make time!" Alec said, "Wait here a moment," and went in the back. He came back and said, "Jacob will meet you at 10:30 in his office over in the receiving center." I said, "OK."

I went home, and it was around nine thirty. I pulled out my Dictaphone and put a fresh tape in it and put it in my inside lapel pocket. At ten fifteen, I walked to Jacob's office. Just before I walked into the receiving center, I pushed the record button on my Dictaphone.

I walked into Jacob's office and said, "Do you stand behind Alec's decision to fire me?" He said, "Yes." I said, "Why, and you picked one hell of a nice day to do it."

Then Jacob said, "I asked Brenda to come down and sit in on our conversation, so I'll give you my reasons then." We sat in silence for twenty minutes. Finally Brenda walked in.

I took over the conversation by saying, "Did you fire me because you think I am anti-Semitic?" Jacob quickly replied, "YES, THAT IS SOMETHING I WILL NOT TOLERATE. I DO NOT TOLERATE IT IN MY FRIENDS OR CHILDREN, EITHER. IT IS SOMETHING YOU CAN NOT CHANGE. THE DAMAGE WAS DONE AT A VERY YOUNG AGE."

"Jacob, all I said to Alec is you and Amber have a bond of faith. Just like I feel a bond with Brenda because we are both Catholic." Brenda, with a horrified look on her face, replied,

"Bill, I do not feel a bond with you because we are both Catholic." "I am sorry you feel that way, Brenda. I have a high opinion of you!" I countered.

"Well, Jacob, if that's you explanation, it's been a pleasure working for you. Thanks for the opportunity you provided me." I stood up, shook his hand, and left.

The irony here is I grew up around Jewish people. Specifically, the Kleins, and Shaun Klein was one of my very best friends.

On my walk home, I thought to myself, "What an elitist, narrow-minded pack of assholes, with the exception of Jacqueline."

I called home and told my mother what had happened. She started laughing and said, "You don't need them, Billy. We will fly you home. I'll call you right back."

Twenty minutes later, my mother called back and said, "Billy, today is a blackout date for frequent flyer miles, but Christmas is not. You're booked on a 9:00 a.m. flight, OK?" "That is fine, Mother. I will see you on Christmas."

I flew to Memphis the next morning.

CHAPTER **28**

Dr. Spencer

I began seeing Dr. Spencer shortly after I started at Pitkin County Dry Goods.

I told him I was having trouble tolerating Lithium, so he lowered my dose and attempted to put me on a high dose of Ativan (Lorazepam). I did not like Ativan and preferred to smoke pot to relieve stress. He was an amateur shrink playing number games and mind games.

Dr. Spencer was a high-profile pill giver to Aspen's elite, with a high opinion of himself.

During one of my sessions, the operators of the Experiment had me lie out loud in my spoken voice and say, "You know Beathan Trading, the firm my father works for, makes a regular practice of backdating orders."

Right after this session, I called my father at work, and I could hear the anger in his voice when he asked, "Where are you?" "At home," I replied.

So, a week later at my next session with Dr. Spencer, I said, "I think your office is bugged!" He chuckled and said, "Not by me, it is not."

Then one day he said, "Maybe we should do a CAT scan and see if it is something other than bipolar. It is, however, very expensive." This statement demonstrates knowledge of the Experiment, and he never gave me the CAT scan.

Whenever I was in Aspen, I was under Dr. Spencer's care, and he never admitted knowledge of the Experiment or lifted a finger to help me.

CHAPTER 29

My Life in Aspen

I spoke with Robert Gallagher, a fraternity brother who lived in Chicago, who told me to look up all of his friends who worked at the Jerome Hotel in Aspen: Adan, Lenard, Ashcraft, Clark, et al. These guys were great to me and made up a large network of my friends. I hung out with them regularly and went to their watering holes with them. They are the ones who orientated me to the part of Aspen I could afford.

Then one day, when I was walking back from City Market Grocery Store to my place, I saw a help-wanted sign in the Durant Street Video Store.

The next morning I applied and got a part-time job. Oscar Corwin was the sole proprietor. Oscar was a super nice guy. I also took a job as a PBX (switchboard operator) at the Grand Aspen Hotel part-time.

Stephanie Wentworth lent me her skiing medallion when she could, so I got to ski once in a while. Stephanie would also have me up once a month for dinner at her place, and she would usually have guests. Stephanie is an excellent cook, and her dinner parties were a blast.

Madeline and Archie Caldwell, a wealthy family from Wichita, would have me over, and I dated their nanny, Kimberly, for a while. Kimberly was from Kansas City. She was a bright, warmhearted, good-looking young woman.

Life was pretty good.

Spring hit, and Oscar Corwin offered me the manager position of the video store. I gladly accepted and quit the PBX job.

Then there was a minor setback: my apartment flooded, and the operators of the Experiment made me get in a huge emotional fight with my landlord, Raymond Marrow. Raymond arranged for an insurance adjustment and claim, and no harm was done.

Outside my regular group of friends, I was always getting off-the-cuff comments from people on the street. This was always a clue that something odd was going on. Aspen made a feeble attempt to play games with me, and everything was shits and giggles because they did not know what I had endured or was about to endure.

Then my father called and said, "You need to take a long road trip." So I drove all over the Rocky Mountain range and was gone for four days. I even unhooked my cell phone in the car at the battery, to ensure I was not being traced.

This cost me my job at the video store and was the beginning of the end of my life in Aspen.

CHAPTER **30**

The Drive to Wichita

With no job, I was bumming around in Aspen, and the operators of the Experiment came up with something for me to do: drive to Wichita as an imaginary cocaine dealer. Not much of a stretch.

I crawled into my BMW, drove over Independence Pass, and arrived on the other side of the range, and the voice said aloud, "You're being tailed by the cops." So I pulled over, got out of the car, opened the hood and unhooked the car phone at the battery again, hopped back in the car, and turned around. I drove ten miles with my eyes peeled for cops and then turned around again.

Then the voice said aloud, "Pick up the coke!" Game on, and I was playing. I spotted an abandoned motel, pulled in, spotted an open doorway, stopped the car, and opened the trunk. I walked through the doorway and back out again and closed the trunk.

I headed toward Pueblo and took the turn to head out across

the plains. I did not need a map—I knew these roads like the back of my hand.

The voice said aloud, "Your contact is going to meet you in Dodge City." Easy. Dodge was about four hours away, but I shaved it to three. I like to drive fast.

I arrived in Dodge and drove to the airport. The voice said aloud, "Your contact will meet you behind hangar three, and your belt and shoes are bugged." I walked down to hangar five, took off my belt and shoes, and walked barefoot back to hangar three and sat down. I waited two hours, while the operators of the Experiment ran all kinds of crazy bullshit through my head.

After waiting two hours, I got tired of the bullshit, and obviously no one was showing up, so I walked back to hangar five and put my shoes and belt back on.

Then the voice said aloud, "Fly the 172 to Wichita. That is your final destination!" I walked up to the tied-down 172 and tried both doors. They were locked, thank god. I do know how to hot-wire a magneto piston airplane.

I got back into the BMW and debated in my mind looking up one of my father's old friends who lived in Dodge, but it was after 1:00 a.m., so I continued to Wichita. It was not that far away.

While I was driving, the operators of the Experiment changed the subject from cocaine to nuclear bombs. This was a new topic for them.

I was tired when I arrived in the wee hours of the morning in Wichita, so I drove to the Wichita Country Club. I knew that there was an overnight guard in the parking lot. Therefore, I pulled up to the groundskeeper's road, opened the gate, drove in, and closed the gate behind me. At two miles per hour, I drove the golf course road up to the back of the tennis court buildings and parked for the night. The operators of the Experiment had me grab a gym sock out of my bag and lie on the hood of the BMW and masturbate into it. When I blew my load, they said aloud, "You launched two missiles on Moscow, kid!"

I crawled back into the BMW, reclined the seat, and went to sleep.

In the morning, some workers flew by in a golf cart and woke me up. So I fired up the BMW, pulled into the parking lot, and drove around to the golf side, where the men's locker room was. I grabbed my bag, went into the locker room, had the attendant open my father's locker, threw my bag in, shit, showered, and shaved. Put fresh clothes on. Walked into the men's grill, sat down, ate breakfast, signed the ticket "Billy Nicholson 1407," picked up the phone, and called my best friend, Arthur Barrows.

"Arthur, Bill Nicholson. I am at the club, and I am thinking of moving to Wichita." "Awesome, Bill. I'm headed to the office. You remember where that is located, don't you?" "Yes." "Give me a couple of hours and then meet me there." "OK, see you soon."

I decided to drive around Wichita for a while until I went to see Arthur. I drove out of the club and made a right on Thirteenth Street as I passed the Beechcraft lakes and the railroad tracks. I floored the BMW got up to 110 miles per hour and locked down the brakes. With the tires smoking, I came to a stop and pushed the hazard button. The voice said aloud, "You launched two more missiles, kid."

I turned around and drove down Thirteenth Street, passed the club on my left, and then passed the Oxberry Estate on my right. The voice said aloud, "Sebastian Oxberry has missiles too and a command center under his house."

I drove around for a bit and then headed to Eastborough, a city inside the city of Wichita (a tax dodge). I drove up Mission Road, past the Loughlins' house (they have a ranch named 777), and looked at a license plate that said, "777." The voice said aloud, "That's a launch code, kid—remember it!" I drove to 3 Peachtree Lane, one of my childhood homes. I had the Eastborough Ecology Club when I lived there.

Enough time had passed, so I headed down to 7 UP bottling, Arthur's and his father's company.

I arrived and went in to see Arthur. Arthur was excited to see me. He extended his hand and gave me a firm handshake and hug, and his father did the same. I sat down and drank RC Cola and discussed with them my plans to relocate to Wichita. Finally, Arthur invited me to stay with him and his new wife and child.

I left 7 UP and headed back to the Club. I took the Canal route to First Street, which headed east one way. When I reached College Hill, there was road construction. There was sand on the roadway and uneven pavement with barrels blocking the center lane for two blocks with no workers or equipment. So, I sped up to sixty miles per hour and slalomed the barrels, with the rear end of the BMW sliding back and forth on the sand. When I finished the two-block stretch of road, I said aloud, "BMW, there is no substitute!!!"

I turned off on Belmont and drove by 401 North Belmont, the second house in which I lived in Wichita.

I pulled into the club and went into the mixed grill and ate lunch. I saw a lot of people I knew from childhood.

I spent my nights at Arthur's house and ate my meals and showered at the club.

One morning I did shower at Arthur's house, and while I was in the shower, the voice said inside my head, "I will let you have my child to experiment on too." This started to clue me in a little. Then I got out of the shower, toweled dry, and brushed my hair and picked up a nail clipper. Again, inside my head the voice said, "When you clip your right pinky nail, it will signal the assassination of the president." I began clipping my left hand first, like I always do, and when I clipped my right pinky nail, the voice said aloud, "You assassinated the president!"

After three nights of staying with Arthur, he informed me that

Jerald Reynolds at Euro-Tech wanted to talk to me. Euro-Tech was a high-end used foreign car dealership. I went and spoke with Jerald, and he offered me a job.

I called my mother and said, "Mother, I'm in Wichita, and I have a job offer with Jerald Reynolds at Euro-Tech. I think I want to move here. What do you think?" "That sounds great, Billy. I'll fly in on Friday and stay with April. Do you want to meet at the club at 1:00 p.m. for lunch, and we can discuss it further?" "Perfect. I love you, Mother. See you then. Bye."

Arthur and I had a great time hanging out.

Friday came, and I met my mother for lunch. My mother said, "Billy, I have been talking to Stephanie Wentworth, and she is leaving Sunday afternoon for ten days for St. Andrews, Scotland, for Grant's graduation. So, we were thinking that I could rent you a U-haul to drive back to Aspen, and you could house-sit for her while you pack up your things, and then you could move here." I replied, "That sounds like a great plan!"

As we finished lunch, Eleanor, the mixed-grill manager, brought the ticket to my mother and thanked her profusely because she knew my parents would pay for all the meals I had eaten all week.

My mother signed the ticket and then asked, "Can you park your car at Arthur's while you're gone?" "I am sure I can. I'll go call him." I got up used the house phone and told Arthur the plan and he OK'd it and even lent me his K40 radar detector.

I came back, sat down, and told my mother, "Arthur said to just swing by in the morning on the way to U-haul." "Great. I have a room for us at Tall Grass Inn for tonight."

Mother and I wondered around town and checked into the inn. She had the private bedroom, and I slept on the pullout couch in the living room. We went to sleep around ten.

I woke up out of a dead sleep around 2:00 a.m. I slid the sliding glass door open to the balcony and closed the door behind me. I stood in pitch blackness in my boxer shorts. I dropped my boxers to my feet and stepped out of them; my dick was already erect. I began masturbating and stepped to the rail. When I blew a huge load over the rail, the voice shouted aloud, "I am a god. No man challenges me. Partake of my sperm—it contains great power to make the master race!!!" This was pretty grandiose stuff. I'm sure any shrink reading this will have a field day.

Then I pissed over the rail, dug around for my boxers, put them back on, and went back to bed.

My mother woke me up around 7:30 a.m. She had already showered and was making coffee, so I grabbed a quick shower and a cup of joe also. She followed me in her rental to Arthur's, and I parked my BMW and retrieved the radar detector from Arthur's, and we drove to U-haul.

She rented the truck on her credit card and gave it to me for gas and incidentals.

We hugged, and I hopped into the truck and headed for Aspen by way of Denver. I was not going to take the U-haul on a single-lane road the whole way or go over Independence Pass.

I had every intention of moving to Wichita when I left. Little did I know what the operators of the Experiment had planned for me.

CHAPTER **31**

House-Sitting for Stephanie

On the drive back to Aspen, the operators of the Experiment continued to speak about nuclear missiles and bombs. I made it to Stephanie's in record time thanks to Arthur's K40 radar detector.

Stephanie was glad to see me. She had some food for me, and we sat up for a while drinking red wine.

Then Stephanie went to bed, and I stepped out on her deck and smoked a joint.

In the morning, Stephanie gave me house-sitting instructions and then left in her jeep to drive to Denver to catch a flight to Scotland.

The operators of the Experiment wasted no time that evening. They started having me play music and masturbate and pee to certain lyrics. I lubricated my dick with olive oil and also lubricated objects to shove up my ass. Everything was very sexual. Every time I came, they told me aloud that I had launched missiles on some destination.

They also said inside my head, "The house is bugged," and had me sing aloud certain lyrics in order to speak to me.

The next evening they had me arrange Stephanie's three oval kerosene candles in a circle and put Arthur's K40 radar detector in the middle and light the candles. Then they played Ziggy Marley's "666" on the stereo and had me sing "666" and then said aloud, "You launched them all." I blew out the candles and smoked another joint on the deck and went to bed.

The next day I drove Nathaniel's (Stephanie's ex-husband) old car down to the town of Aspen. I walked into the record store, and facing me inside the door on the sale rack was U2 WAR. Aspen was playing along too; everyone knew! I bought the album.

I went back up to Stephanie's and the operators of the Experiment had a great time with U2 WAR that night. Complete with masturbation and singing aloud. They kept me up really late.

The next day I slept until four in the afternoon. I woke up feed Kitty, who was starving by then. When nightfall came, the operators of the Experiment stripped me naked, walked me out on the deck, and sat me down in the lounge chair. The first thing I did was get high. I had taken the bottle of olive oil out with me. I lubed up and masturbated for a long time, and just before I came, I stopped stroking and let my dick go limp. About twenty minutes later, I got erect again. I stroked hard and long and just before cumming, I let my dick go limp again. I was sitting in the darkness under the stars and in the moonlight. I jacked off two more times without cumming. Finally, with a stiff dick, I walk back into house. I got my Shetland signature St. Andrews sweater and put it on. I walked back out on the deck, lay back down on the lounge chair, and relubed my dick. Kitty was sitting at my side. She is a Manx from the Isle of Man. The operators made some kind of a comment about missiles and the Isle of Man. Then I began stroking my dick with tremendous force, and five minutes later blew a gusher load all over myself. The operators of the Experiment shouted aloud, "YOU BLEW AWAY SCOTLAND."

I lay there exhausted for about an hour and then smoked a joint. I lounged for about another thirty minutes under the stars and moon. Then I got up and went inside, ripped off my sweater, and crawled into the shower. I took a twenty-minute hot shower and then turned the water cold for five minutes.

When I was towel-drying off, I was pretty sure something strange was going on with me, but I still did not have the full picture.

I went to sleep.

I woke up late again the next day. As I was having coffee, the operators of the Experiment said, "WICHITA SUCKS, KID. WE ARE NOT GOING THERE. PREP THE HOUSE—WE ARE GOING ON A TRIP!!!

Then they took over. I overwatered the plants. I grabbed Kitty and put her in Nathaniel's car and drove to the vet. When I got to the vet, she knew where she was and got away from me. I grabbed her, and she scratched the shit out of my arms. The people at the vet had me put her in the cage. I drove back up to Stephanie's. I packed my things and crawled into the empty U-haul.

The operators said aloud, "Head to your grandmother's in Denver."

So, I was helpless, driving an empty U-haul to Denver.

CHAPTER **32**

The Trip Across the Water

While I was driving from Aspen to Vail, all the chatter in my brain was about nuclear missiles and bombs.

Then I drove into the Eisenhower Tunnel, and the voice inside my head said, "Where should I go? Jamaica?" Then the voice shouted aloud, "I KNOW. I'LL GO TO ST. ANDREWS."

Again I had no choice, but why fight it? St. Andrews sounded fun. They were controlling me, and I did not know I was being controlled, but I was not actively trying to fight it. This made it easy on them. The only explanation I had been given by anyone was that I was bipolar and subject to episodes. This certainly qualified.

I arrived at my grandmother's place in Denver and parked the truck out front.

I rang the bell to my grandmother's apartment, and she asked, "Who is it?" "Billy." "Oh, Billy, come right in," and she buzzed me in. She fixed me a sandwich, and we chatted for a while.

Then we went to bed. I was in the guest bedroom. I watched *Star Trek* on TV. Then I got up and walked around the house, and the clocks were all set to different times. I went to the kitchen and pulled out a large, sharp carving knife and went back into the guest bedroom and lied down. I held the knife with both hands at the top of abdomen just below my rib cage in a stabbing position, and the voice said aloud, "Do you want to end it all now, kid?" I held the knife there for about fifteen minutes and got up and put it away back in the kitchen.

Then the voice said, over and over in my head, "Why don't you fuck your grandmother, kid," and then I fell asleep in the bed.

In the morning, my grandmother woke me up early. I took a shower, and she served me toast with butter and jelly and coffee.

I gave her a hug and told her I loved her and got in the U-haul.

I drove the U-haul truck to Stapleton Airport, double-parked the truck in the departure lane, and went in and bought a ticket to London on Northwest on my mother's credit card.

I came out, crawled in the truck, and drove right to a U-haul rental return agency. This proves that the operators were driving the truck. I parked the truck and walked in with the paperwork. The agent told me how much it would be, and I handed him my mother's credit card, and it declined. He said, "that's OK—we can force charge it!" I asked him to call me a cab, and he did.

The cab arrived. I crawled in and said, "Stapleton, Northwest, International." Something you should know is I always carry my passport. It's an old habit!

It was not a direct flight to London; I connected through Boston. I checked in well in advance of the two-hour requirement for international flights. I showed the check-in agent my passport and ticket and went through security. I grabbed a snack on the concourse and waited for my flight to Boston.

I boarded, and we flew to Boston.

In Boston I walked down the concourse and checked in at the London gate. I said, "It's a little balmy, I'd say," as I handed my ticket to a large, fat black man; he laughed. Everyone seemed to be having a good time with me, and I was not sure why.

I boarded the plane, stowed my small bag in the overhead bin, and sat down. We sat on the tarmac for two hours because of a mechanical delay. The operators of the Experiment said inside my head, "There is a bomb on the plane." I was not going to fall for that after all the nuclear discussion. Finally, we pulled away from the gate. The stewardesses gave the safety spiel. The operators said in my head, "You don't have to comply with FAA regulations." So I did not wear my safety belt, and I did not get any flak from the flight attendants about it. Then the operators told me that everything they were saying people could hear on their in-flight headsets. Then they started in my head. "Life is an illusion; imagery is a bitch." "Life even at its very worst is still worth living." "I never lie; I always tell the truth. I always lie; I never tell the truth. A paradox." "FAA vs.

FCC [who legally controls a broadcast to your head on an airplane]." "NRA vs. IRA." "You should have your FAA medical. Your vision is excellent; your health is excellent." "The plane is actually being hijacked to Germany not London." And so on. Finally we were on final approach to London.

We landed in London.

CHAPTER 33

The Trip to St. Andrews

Once in London, I tried to rent a car on my mother's credit card. I was unsuccessful. Therefore, I exchanged half of my money.

So I hopped a commuter flight to Glasgow. We took off, and the voice inside my head started again. "The kingdom of Bill." "Where is Wales anyway?" Then the discussion was about foreign employment and the limit of a US passport.

We were on final approach when the captain said over the PA, "We have arranged a rental car with !@#$%^&*." The company name was garbled. Then, as clear as a bell: "Alamo." We touched down. This seemed very strange to me, direct help, but what the hell, I thought, I'll give it a try. As I exited the plane, the first officer winked at me.

I went to Alamo for a rental car and handed the agent my mother's credit card, my passport, and my driver's license. He said, "Here you go, Mr. Williamson. You're all set." I said, "My name is Nicholson, and I want insurance." He said, "I need your surname," smiled and handed me my paperwork and directed me to the car. "You're all set. Let me know if you have any problems with the radio." So I walked out to the car.

I am named after my grandfather's father, William, or Bill, who came to the United States from Scotland. I guess I was home.

The car they gave me was a black Volkswagen Golf with a manual transmission. I got in and started off for St. Andrews. And of course the radio did not work.

The operators of the Experiment were driving. I headed straight to St. Andrews.

The voice was singing out loud, "Jukebox hero. He heard one guitar, just blew him away. Couldn't get a ticket—it was a sold-out show." "Abracadabra, I'm going to reach out and grab you." They also played games with billboards and license plates.

I arrived in St. Andrews in the late afternoon and drove around for a while.

CHAPTER 34

The Night of Fear and Enlightenment

I parked the car and walked the streets.

I went to the bank and exchanged some British pounds for German marks and crumpled a US twenty-dollar bill and threw it in the trash. The voice said inside my head, "Good job, laundryman!"

Then I walked down to Kate's bar and had one beer. The barmaid asked if I wanted ice, and I said, "No, I'll drink it warm."

I left the bar and went to a street vendor and ordered fish and chips. I crossed the street and sat down on the sidewalk with my back leaning against Woolrich, the department store, and ate dinner.

Then I checked into a B and B, # 10 Gate House, in St. Andrews. I tried to use my mother's credit card, but the innkeeper would only accept cash. He gave me a really nice room at the top of the stairs, number four, with a private bath down the hall. While I was checking in, the voice inside my head said, "He does not know he is in the presence of greatness!"

I settled into the room and took a shower. While I was taking a shower, the voice made a big deal about wasting water. So I got wet, shut the water off, lathered up, and then rinsed off. I toweled dry and put on a Giorgio Armani shirt and khakis.

I took a walk around St. Andrews that evening. The place was basically abandoned. Graduation had taken place one day prior to my arrival.

I was fascinated by an old graveyard. I looked over a short concrete wall at the headstones in the night mist and seemed to hallucinate a little. The voice was discussing aloud Germany and Switzerland. "Swiss are basically Germans in sheep's clothing and too neutral to trust."

Still tripping, I walked down to the wharf and water's edge. It was low tide, and the boats were sitting in mud in the harbor. It was a dark, steamy, brisk night. The fog provided limited visibility of the sea. Voices in the distance were shouting, "Yes, apartheid bashing." Then the operators of the Experiment started shouting out to sea, "Look into the 'ID' and release the beast. Welcome to the kingdom of Bill. I am a god. No one is more capable of destroying the World Bank than me. The power of three. No man is worthier than I am. I stare into the abyss and laugh at thee."

I strongly questioned my diagnosis during this oral conversation and had a feeling of being totally controlled.

I walked back to #10 Gate House and passed by a house with a British flag in the window blasting opera music.

When I arrived at the B and B, I crawled into bed and turned on the TV. *The White Room* was on. I watched for a while, and when the boy pulled off his shirt and picked up a bouquet of roses, I said, "I bet he's going to thrash his back with the thorns." I had already seen the movie. I bet I confused the operators a little.

I was still believing I was constantly bugged and now controlled, and the real freak show was about to begin.

Suddenly, the voices inside my head said, "Who said that?" "Who said that?" "Who said that?" "Who said that?" This bantering back and forth went on for about ten minutes. Then they did the same bantering back and forth in my external voice for ten minutes. Then they said inside my head for about ten minutes, "Who said that?" This was followed by them saying in my external voice, "Who said that?" Then they bantered inside and out for about another ten minutes. I was catching on quickly, overcome with fear and curiosity.

My heart was beating faster and faster and faster.

Then they switched to "Who are we?" They bantered back and forth internally and externally for another ten minutes.

"ARE WE NASA?" "ARE WE CIA?" "ARE WE MILITARY?" They bantered back and forth internally and externally for another ten minutes.

"THE ASSASSIN IS HERE. STAY PUT!!!!!!!"

Freaking out, I went to the bathroom and took a monster shit of fear. Then the voice started to speak to me aloud (in my spoken voice). I leaned forward on the head and grabbed my dopp kit and took out a bottle of Lithium, popped the lid, and put a tablet on my tongue. Then, with tremendous force, the operators spit it out and said, "Stop taking those. They will not help you!!!"

I sat there experiencing some relief knowing that I was not crazy but subject to experimentation. At this point, I truly understood what was going on and how powerless I truly was. I wiped my ass and walked back into the bedroom.

The operators of the Experiment decided to prove a point. They walked me over to the fourth-story window and cranked it open, and I threw one leg out. I was sitting there straddling the frame when they said, "LIFE, EVEN AT ITS VERY WORST, IS STILL WORTH LIVING, BUT PEOPLE SHOULD HAVE A CHOICE!!!!"

Fear set in again.

Then the operators said, "Seriously, kid, if you jumped, you might break a leg or fracture a skull, but you're not going to die. WAIT. THE ASSASSIN IS HERE!!!" I got out of the window and shut it and crawled back into bed.

I finally got to sleep as the sun was coming up.

The young houseboy came into my room around 10:00 a.m. and got linens from an overhead closet in my room and said, "It is time for breakfast and checkout." I went back to sleep. Finally, the innkeeper came up at 11:15 and said, "If you don't leave in the next fifteen minutes, I'll have to charge you another day." I grabbed my things and left.

This was probably the scariest night of my life, but from that day forward I have been truly enlightened.

CHAPTER 35

Getting Back to London

I found the rental car on the street and drove to a callbox. I inserted enough change to get an international operator, but no matter what I tried, the phone would not work. I walked back to the car and got into the wrong side—I was sitting in the passenger side. This was the first time I had made that mistake. I got out, walked around the car and got behind the wheel, and drove to another callbox. No luck, again. Then the voice said aloud, "Stop trying, kid. You cannot call the States!"

So, I decided to drive to Glasgow. But the operators of the Experiment said, "We're headed to Edinburgh." Therefore, with a raging headache and racing thoughts, I felt the operators head me toward Edinburgh.

"Your two hemispheres of the brain are at war, kid," the operators explained as they fired neurons in rapid sequences. "Monarchy vs. Democracy." "Nuclear holocaust—US targets have been hit." "The assassin is coming at you." Then a bus passed me, with a blond-haired, blue-eyed man with wire-rim glasses standing in the stairwell of the front window; he looked like he was right out of a movie.

As we passed through towns, the operators kept bouncing the front left tire off of curbs. Finally, when I was back on the rural highway, I got a flat. I pulled off onto the grass and changed the tire.

We drove right past the turn for Edinburgh and Annan, and the voice said aloud, "Sorry, kid, you do not get to see your relatives; we're going to Glasgow." Then they kept driving me around in circles. I kept ending up at the same rotary near a fire station. Finally, I pulled into the fire station. Two firemen walked out and said, smiling, "Are you over here on vacation?" I responded, somewhat distressed, "I guess. How do I get to Glasgow?" Their smiles dropped, and they were very kind and gave me directions.

I rolled into the Glasgow airport in late afternoon. It was pouring down rain. I asked two uniformed policemen out front, "When is the next flight to London?" One answered, "Not until tomorrow." "How do I get to London?" "Follow the M3 road signs. They will lead you there. Sorry, sir, but we cannot help over here. Go home!!!!" "I am going back to the States." "Excellent." And each policeman gave me a thumbs-up. Naturally, the operators drove me in the wrong direction.

Night fell upon the countryside, and I was tired, so I pulled into a roadside restaurant parking lot, reclined the car seat, and went to sleep.

THE EXPERIMENT: AMERICA'S INSANITY BY DESIGN

In the morning I went in to use the restroom. As I sat on the toilet, the voice started, aloud: "As you slept, we downloaded your brain's information into a computer. You did well against a man; now try a computer." Then the voice fired off all my neurons and ran so many thoughts through my brain I could not keep up; my head ached, and my stomach felt like it was going to explode. "We also installed bombs in your stomach while you slept. You're a complete assassin now!" I freaked out on the toilet for a good half hour while shit poured out of me. Finally, I got up, wiped my ass, and got back into the car. I was not hungry.

We drove east along the coast from Dumfries. The operators began to discuss Ireland. "Imagine an Irish Catholic boy teaming up with the IRA. We're going to catch a ferry to Ireland." We did not catch a ferry, thank god. And the operators we're heading me in the right direction.

I spotted a sign for M3 and hopped on the highway. The voice started in, aloud: "Nick vs. the computer. Is it live or is it Memorex? We taped your dreams last night. We'll play them back. Don't worry—we're driving." Then my imagination went wild with visual images, like daydreams, for a good two hours. Finally, it stopped. "What did you think of that, kid? Pretty trippy!!!"

We pulled to a roadside restaurant, and I went in and ate beans, wienies, and bread. Then I got back out on the highway.

"Now, kid, the war of the two hemispheres of the brain, again; you need the practice!" They shot neurons from one side to the other in multitude of patterns. My head was aching. And they spoke inside and out. "War vs. peace." "Piped-in thoughts vs. dreams." "Freedom vs. a caged mind." "They [the two hemispheres of the brain] want to be together." "Human operator vs. a computer." "Who are you? Who are we?" "Who said that? Who said that?" "Billy and Billy (Billy squared)." And so on. Finally we arrived in London, and they stopped. We had driven through the night.

I drove around London, lost.

The operators of the Experiment were obviously driving, so I let them drive. We pulled into a neighborhood, and a young boy cleaned my windshield as I sat at a traffic light. He finished, and I gave him a US twenty-dollar bill. He looked at it and got a strange look on his face and held it up as I drove away; I doubt he had ever seen one before.

We drove up and down streets, and I spotted a parking place. I parallel parked. I got out and sat down on the hood. The voice started inside my head. "Another US target destroyed, Texas, and it's your fault." Then I looked up at the billboard on top of a building. It was an ice cream ad; the caption was "Silky Smooth." The operators said inside, "Take off your shirt." I did and put it on the hood beside me. "You're silky smooth, kid. Keep your dick!"

Two men were unloading a large mirror off of a truck from across the street and crossed and passed right in front of me. I saw my reflection in the mirror. I thought of "The Man in the Mirror" from my Sigma Chi days at college. I began to cry as the men carried the mirror into an antiques retail shop. I had a good cry, put on my shirt, and got back into the car.

The operators drove me back out onto the highway again. Then we pulled into another neighborhood surrounded with a concrete wall with barbed wire on top. The voice spoke out loud again. "This was a World War II concentration camp. This is where we conducted human experiments. The technology used here could have birthed what's happening to you today. Now it is run by the Mob." As we made a turn past a grocery store, there was an Italian-looking man leaning in the doorway smoking a cigarette (a strange coincidence).

We pulled out of the neighborhood onto highway M11. A motorcycle zoomed by, and the voice said aloud, "Does Soc Gen [Society General] mean anything to you? OK, no reason it should."

Finally, we arrived at an airport, Stansted not Heathrow. I pulled in and looked for an Alamo car rental return. Then the voice said, "Don't worry. Park the car anywhere—it doesn't matter. Remember, you were never over here. The car was rented under the name Williamson." I parked the car on the second story of the parking garage, section B. I gathered up everything outside the car, paperwork, luggage, and currency. Then I took a towel out of my bag and wiped away finger-prints on the steering wheel, dash, stick shift, seat belt, seats, center console, and inside windshield and then locked the door. Then I wiped down the door and door handle on both sides, tail gate, and hood. I finished by wiping down the key and left it on the front right tire. I gathered my things and went into the airport. The voice said inside my head, "You'd make a good spy!"

I went up to the American counter and said, "Do you have any flights left to the States?" and handed them my passport and my mother's credit card. The credit card was declined, and the agent said, "I'm sorry. Do you have another form of payment?" While this was going on, the agents at the desk next to American said loud enough for me to hear, "Virgin will do it!!!!" So I asked the American agent for my mother's credit card and passport back and walked down to Virgin Airways.

I walked up to the Virgin Airway's counter and said, "Do you have any flights to the States?" "We have a flight to New York in thirty minutes." "Can I still get on it? Here is my passport and credit card." I watched as the machine said, "Declined," but the ticket printed. The agent said, "Here you go, Mr. Nicholson, have a pleasant trip." "Thank you so much, ma'am."

I went straight to the bank and exchanged all my money for US currency and boarded the plane. As I boarded, a large group of Indian people clapped.

Once on the plane, I put my bag in the overhead bin and sat down in my seat.

I remember thinking that only MI6 could have given me the education I received in the United Kingdom. Total body control, speech control, thought control, and brain control. I was ready to go home!!!!!!

CHAPTER 36

The Flight to NYC

I had a window seat. We pulled away from the gate and sat on a taxiway.

We were on the taxiway for a long time, and the voice tried to convince me that all of the international planes taxiing by were saying good-bye to me.

Then the voice on the inside said, "Get ready, kid—we're going to blow up an empty plane for you," and then shut up and had me stare out the window for about ten minutes. "You know better, kid. Obviously we're not going to blow up a plane." I laughed out loud. My spirits were fairly decent.

"Remember, kid, the head honcho of Virgin Airways is a friend of yours—he's sending you home!!!! He'll always help you out if you need a friend!!!" the voice informed me inside my head. "Get some sleep—you need it!"

So, I took a three-hour nap.

I woke with a headache, and the voice said, "The United States and the United Kingdom are fighting over control of you in international waters." The voice then began to mock England, Scotland, and the Queen.

Then a passenger came up to the passenger seated next to me and said, "Be quiet; you're seated right next to him, and we cannot hear the music." Enough bullshit from the peanut gallery. I rolled my eyes and went back to sleep.

I managed to sleep until we hit US airspace and I was forced out of a dead sleep.

The voice said, "You're back in US airspace," and I got up from my seat and pulled my small bag from the overhead bin and took out everything I had acquired from the United Kingdom. I zipped it shut and put it back in the overhead bin. I sat down in my seat and put everything in the seat pocket in front of me. Then I examined myself (pockets, etc.) and put the rest of the UK stuff in the seat pocket as well. I remember thinking I should have ditched the stuff in London, but this was the next best thing. I held onto my ticket for customs, and that was it.

Then the operators piped in a headache—nothing sophisticated, like a neuron-firing headache, just pain. And they said, "A horse is a horse, of course. They call me Mr. Ed." "A horse is a horse, of course. They call me Mr. Bill." Over and over again, until we landed. Then they piped in tears. So I was crying, listening to bullshit with a headache.

The stewardess came up and asked, "Are you OK?" "Yes," I replied and thought to myself, "Ain't it grand to be back in the country that experiments on me!!! In the hands of amateurs!!!!!"

I sucked up the tears.

Then the stewardess brought the customs cards down the aisle. The operators said, "Don't fill that out!"

We finally landed.

As I was getting off the plane, still having the headache, the voice said over and over again in my head, "New York, New York, what a wonderful town, where the people ride in a hole in the ground." What a pack of idiots at the controls.

I got to customs and the black customs agent was a real jerk. He said, "What do you expect me to do with this? Fill out and go to the back of the line." So I did. I finally cleared customs. I stood in line for a cab. Finally, when I got in the cab, the operators stopped repeating, "New York, New York, what a wonderful town, where the people ride in a hole in the ground."

I told the cabby, "Take me to the Plaza Hotel, top of the park, in Manhattan." He shook his head and said, "Where do you want to go?" "The Plaza." He pulled out and hit his brakes a few times, and the operators of the Experiment said, "Give us a break, kid!"

CHAPTER 37

The Night in NYC (Manhattan)

We arrived at the Plaza, and I paid the cabbie most of the rest of my money. I walked in and went to the front desk and handed the clerk my mother's credit card. It was declined, and I inquired about the possibility of writing a check. The clerk said that she would need another form of payment.

So I left the Plaza and walked west to the next hotel, the Park Lane. I went to the front desk and asked, "Can I have someone call in a credit card for me to stay here for the night?" She informed me that they would require a Xerox copy of an ID and credit card with a signature faxed to the hotel to check in.

Then the bellhop asked, "Would you like me to hold your bag?" I said, "That would be great," and he handed me a claim stub. I handed him my bag and a five-dollar bill and said, "Thanks." He smiled and put my bag in the bellman's closet.

I walked over to the pay phone and tried to call my parents with my memorized calling card. But my fingers were not working. After the fourth try, I said aloud, "Oh, that's cute." Then the operators inside my head said, "OK, we will let you call them." This time I successfully dialed, and my father answered. "Dad, I'm in New York at the Park Lane, and I need you to fax in an ID and credit card for a night stay!" "Billy, that's much too expensive. You need to go to the Swiss Hotel." "Well, Dad, I am out of money and very confused. Can you please put me up here just one night until we figure something out?" "Tough. You'll have to sleep in the street, if you cannot make an effort." "Fine, I'll sleep in Harlem." CLICK.

Then I tried to page Barrows. I waited by the phone for forty-five minutes, but he never called back.

While I was waiting, a couple of pros got off the elevator and went to the front desk. The voice said, "Kid, do you want one or both? You can have them!" The pros left the hotel.

Since Arthur did not call me back, I got on the elevator and got off a few floors up. I tried a few doors to see if any were unlocked. No luck.

I took the stairs down to the lounge, which was closed. Went behind the bar and stole a can of Sprite and drank it. While I was drinking it, the janitor came in and vacuumed.

So I took the service elevator to the basement. The voice said as I got off the elevator, "You're in the bowels of the hotel."

I went into the employee bathroom and sat down and tried to take a shit. I was constipated. Then the operators said aloud,

"Don't you hate this when we don't let you shit?" So I pushed even harder. Then they said aloud, "OK, we'll let you shit," and it came gushing out. I got up and wiped my ass, while they said aloud, "Who taught you to reverse wipe anyway, your mother?" Again, amateur games.

I left the hotel and walked on the east side of the park to the Leash Club (the place Benjamin Oxby put me up when I interviewed with the Tudor Group) and rang the bell. No one answered because it was the middle of the night.

The operators took the opportunity to tell me that asking my mother what the name of our Irish setter was, when they had told me at Charter Hospital that they had killed my parents, was a good check. They did this because two cast-iron setters are at the gates leading up to the Leash Club.

I left the Leash Club and walked south (north?) along Central Park toward Washington Square Park.

The operators of the Experiment had me fixate on a billboard Tommy Hilfiger underwear ad.

"Tommy, who figured?" "Tommy Hilfiger vs. Tommy, who figured?" "Tommy Hilfiger vs. Tommy Nelson (my childhood neighbor)." Vivid sexual images were piped in. "We know you always wanted him." And every time I passed these ads, they would say, "Tommy vs. Tommy," and pipe in sexual images. Finally, after I had seen multiple ads they said, "Tommy vs. Tom MacLeod (my uncle)." "You're both bipolar."

"OK, kid, it's 1965, and you're at the Merc, and you're Tom MacLeod—start trading." "If you're back in time, you know what happens in the future—you control the world!" Then the operators had me walk along doing arb signals and yelling out market orders. I am sure I looked insane to any passersby. And they certainly did not make me believe I was controlling any market movements globally. Amateurs!!!!!

Then they took me up to an ATM and inserted my card, and I had a zero balance. "Leave your deposit slip there, kid. People will take you to the $9,999s—they'll put money in your account." I knew full well no one was going put money in my account. Amateurs!!!!

Next they discussed the corruption of the exchange. "*Brokers, Bagmen, and Moles*, kid—you're not a mole. You have to know you're bugged to be a mole. Or maybe you were the perfect mole, someone who was bugged and did not know it. You're not a mole, kid."

I arrived at Washington Square Park. "Didn't you buy pot here, when you stayed with Benjamin Oxby and his girlfriend?" the voice queried. "Pretend to roll a joint and smoke it, kid!" and that is what they did next. They took my hands and rolled a joint and then put it up to my lips and took drags. They were kind enough to pipe in some psychedelia. Finally they were operating the controls with some expertise.

Then, still slightly tripping, I looked across the park at NYU. They said, "Would you like to get a master's at NYU?" This seemed plausible and interesting.

I walked a little farther to Canal Street, and then everyone on the street yelled, "Whoa." I stopped dead in my tracks and looked across the intersection. I saw rundown houses with the Hudson River in the background, so I turned right and began walking again.

Then the operators of the Experiment informed me that they had another subject they were experimenting on, and he was in the control room. They further informed me that our two brains were directly hooked up, saying, "You have done well against the machine, kid. Now try a human brain direct link." I did not buy it, but at least they were getting somewhat creative. They said, "Everything you think of or see, he thinks or sees in his head, and vise versa."

Then they ran a visual image of the L. A. Connection, a homosexual club in my old neighborhood in Wrigleyville in Chicago. "You know you used to frequent the L. A. Connection in Chicago," and they piped in images of a bar with men everywhere having sex. Then a smoking-hot black girl came walking out of a club I passed on the street and said to me, "No, you did not. You always just walked by!!!"

I walked into a corner store and asked the clerk, "Can I please buy a rubber?" and pointed to a condom behind the counter. He said, "Fuck that. Buy a lottery ticket!" Probably good advice but I left the store empty-handed.

I crossed the street, and a beautiful blond-haired, blue-eyed babe crossed in front of me. The voice said inside, "Fuck her. Rape her brains out on top of the trunk of that car in front of everyone. OK, I'll do it," and then they ran an intense detailed mental image of me raping this young girl on the trunk of a car. "Did you enjoy our in lab subject, rape of the girl?"

Then they said, "Enough of using the other subject. We're working alone with you again, kid. The money is in the bag! The money is in the bag! THE MONEY IS IN THE BAG!!!!"

I walked about ten blocks north and came to a city bench and sat down. There was a small park behind me with trees, and across the street I was facing was a private parking garage.

I sat there for about thirty minutes as the high from the imaginary joint wore off.

Then a man approached and asked, "Is this your bench?" "No, you're welcome to sit here." The voice said inside my head, "He's one of us, kid." The man asked, "What are you doing here?" I replied, "Just enjoying the night air." Police cars begin to pass every five minutes. This put me on guard, and I'm thankful NYPD was looking after me!!!! "What do you do for a living?" the man asked. "I am a commodities broker." The voice then chimed in, inside my head, "Be careful, kid— he's not with us!!!" "So," I thought to myself, "this guy might be a homosexual trying to pick me up." "Do you work here in town?" the man asked, a definite pickup line. "No, Chicago." We sat for about another five minutes in silence; he lost interest and stood up. Walking away, he said, "Enjoy your time in New York."

I fell asleep for a brief spell on the bench. I woke to cars coming out of the garage. The voice said aloud, "Kid, we took you to a hospital and did research on you while you slept and returned you to this bench twenty-four hours later the next day." I did not buy it!

Then the newspapers we're being delivered and the operators said, "You're in the morning news," but would not let me get up and check the paper.

The sun was coming up, so I got up and walked back to Manhattan.

I arrived at the Hilton and walked in and tried my mother's credit card and tried to talk my way in—no luck. As I was walking out, I saw a light buffet table, so I grabbed a bagel and cream cheese and a banana. Then a lady from the other side of the lobby came over and rang up the charges at a cash register I had not seen. I had just enough cash to cover it. I sat down in the lobby and ate.

The security guard from the Hilton came over and asked, "What are you doing here?" "I am waiting for a friend." Remember, I had not shaved or showered since St. Andrews. I'm sure I looked like a vagrant. The security guard said, "I'll have to ask you to leave, or I'll have to call the police." "I told you I am waiting for a friend. I have every right to sit here; besides, I just ate your buffet and paid for it." "What's your friend's name?" "Arthur Barrows." He left. A few minutes later he returned and said, "We do not have a reservation for any-one named Arthur Barrows." "It's probably under the corpo-ration name." "What's the corporation name?" "I forget. It is a soft-drink bottling company." He reached out for me. "You better not touch me unless you want to get sued. Go ahead and call the cops!!!!" "Well, you can't sleep here." "Who said anything about sleep? I told you I waiting for a friend, but I doubt he'll stay here after the way you have treated me." "Well, you can't sleep here." "I know." He left again.

The voice said inside my head, "Stand your ground, kid. You're both uptown and downtown at the same time, your Manhattan and Harlem rolled into one. You look like a bum, but you're wearing Giorgio Armani, and you speak the Queen's English. Hold your ground."

A young man dressed very corporate was sitting across from me crying. The voice said inside, "That's the other subject, kid. Stay in New York and trade. Your bank is right across the street. Go apply for a loan."

I looked across the lobby, and a well-dressed Italian family was seated there. The voice said, "Kid, those are the real Mob. They are here to take you to the Vatican in Rome. Do you want to run the Vatican Bank? Here's your chance!"

I had heard enough and overstayed my welcome. I got up and left the Hilton.

As I walked outside, the voice said aloud, "TRY THE PLAZA AGAIN. I BET YOU GET IN THIS TIME!!!"

I walked to the top of Central Park and walked up Park Avenue to the Plaza. I walked past the 999 building and remembered going to Zegna in this building, when I attended the "Collective" at the Plaza on a buying trip for Brick's as a young man.

But all the operators could come up with was, "Flip it over, kid: '999'-'666,' the anti-Christ. Oops, you just launched a missile on Washington, DC."

I walked into the Plaza and got stares from everyone.

CHAPTER 38

The Plaza

I walked up to the front desk and said, "I would like a room, please." The kind lady clerk replied, "What kind of a room?" "Just a standard." "That will be $253." "OK" I did not bat an eye at the price. The manager overheard me and came over and said, "We really did not know, sir. Really, we did not know! How would you like to pay for the room?" "Can I write a check?" "Do you have a credit card to guarantee it?" "Yes." "Then a check will be fine." "Do you want it written on my Chicago or my Aspen account?" "It really doesn't matter." The manager walked away. Again the kind woman asked, "What kind of a room?" "A standard will be fine." "I'll give you a nice, quiet standard room." "Thanks. I will go ahead and write the check for three hundred, in case I incur extra charges." I wrote the check and handed it to her along with my mother's credit card.

I took the elevator up to my room and thought to myself, "Someone arranged my check-in on a rubber check and cooked credit card." THANK YOU!!!!

The first thing I did was order room service, remembering it was morning. I ordered a healthy portion of the breakfast menu. Then I checked out the room and lay down on the bed. Luxury, finally. Fifteen minutes later, there was a knock at the door. I inquired, "Who is it?" "Room service."

The voice piped inside my head said, "He's a British secret service agent sent to kill you. Be careful, kid." I opened the door. The waiter had a big smile and wheeled in breakfast. The voice said, "I told you, kid. He even looks British." I signed the check and left a heavy tip. The waiter looked at the ticket and made eye contact and said, "Right on. Thanks." He closed the door behind him. I inhaled breakfast. It was delicious. British agent, my ass. If England was going to kill me, they would have done it over there.

When I finished breakfast, the operators told me there was a bomb on the food cart. So, for insurance, I rolled it down the hall and around the corner from my room and closed the hall fire doors behind me.

I stripped down to my boxers, went into the bathroom took a shit, and crawled into the very comfortable bed and crashed hard.

I woke up in the middle of the night. The first thing the operators had me do was go over to the light switch and flash the lights off and on in Morse code, SOS, several times. Then they walked me over to the deep window bay. They had me step up and stand in it. They walked me out to the edge of the window and said aloud, "If you jump here, kid, you won't break a leg or crack your skull—you'll DIE!!!!" I was at least twenty floors up. Then they walked me back and forth in the window bay facing the street below. I had the feeling that there were two operators with two separate machines controlling me. One trying to save me and one trying to kill me!!! This went on for twenty minutes, while they said aloud, "TIME TO DIE!!!" over and over again. Finally, they said aloud, "THE MONEY IS IN THE BAG, KID. IT IS GOING TO BE A DIFFICULT, TOUGH, LONG RIDE, BUT WE WILL GIVE YOU $200 MILLION FOR YOUR TROUBLE, OR DO YOU WANT TO END IT NOW?" Then they froze me up against the glass. A few minutes later, they walked me backward, and I jumped out of the bay.

I stood in the room looking out the window and saw the F. O. A. Schwarz sign, and it made me think of Abbie Klein, and the Kleins were the only people I knew in New York City. This was a little calming, as my pounding heart was slowly coming to a resting rate.

Then the voice said, "Call your mother, kid." I dialed my parents. My mother answered. "Mother, I think I had an episode." She asked, "Where are you?" "At the Plaza in Manhattan. I only paid for one night. Can you call and give them a credit card?" "Are you O K?" "NO." "What is the number there, and what's your room number?" I told her. She said, "I'll call you right back."

She called back twenty minutes later. The phone rang. "Hello." "Billy." "Yes." "Tiffany Klein is going to come see you. Is that OK?" "Yes, I think I can discern her." Then the operators of the Experiment piped in my mind, "It's not really your mother, kid," while in my spoken voice, they asked my mother, "How did I get this scare on my forehead? Did Tom MacLeod give it to me?" I was not falling for any of their tricks, but I'm sure it alarmed my mother.

I crawled back into bed to take a nap while I waited for Tiffany. Just before I went to sleep, the operators tried to convince me of some bullshit that I had been moved to the Vatican in my sleep and the view out the window was false. I went to back to sleep.

I was awakened by a knock at the door. I got up and put on my shirt and pants and inquired, "Who is it?" Then a voice from behind me in the bathroom said, "Tiffany." "Oh, that's cute," I said aloud and opened the door. Standing there was Tiffany, a sight for sore eyes.

Tiffany came in and immediately began speaking about our family ski trips to Aspen when we bought out the Apple Jax and stayed there with all our friends. This small talk immediately brought me out of any psychological difficulties planted by the operators. Remember, I had not spoken to anyone I knew in the last few days. Tiffany was a comfort from childhood. After about an hour, there was another knock at the door, and Tiffany answered it. It was Abbie Klein and her boyfriend.

Tiffany and Abbie took the menu in the room and ordered me some more food. The conversation got even more lighthearted, and I was even almost relaxed. The food arrived, and Abbie insisted I eat everything.

Then there was another knock at the door, and in walked Shaun Klein, one of my best friends from childhood. Shortly after that, Tiffany's husband showed up. The room was full, and the conversation was rolling.

The operators of the Experiment were lost; the spook show was over; the home team had arrived. Tiffany's husband said, "There is room for you!" referring to his travel agency business. And the operators tried to pipe in, "There is room for you in the Jewish faith," but I had no trouble ignoring them.

It was getting pretty late, and Abbie's boyfriend and Tiffany's husband left. That left just the Klein children, and we talked for another hour. Then Tiffany and Abbie retired to a room across the hall they had reserved. That left Shaun and me. "Shaun, do you remember the religious discussions we used to have?" "Yes, Bill, it's been a long time since I have had a serious conversation." We sat up and chatted for a while, and then I asked, "Aren't you going to sleep with your sisters?" "No, Bill, I'm going to sleep right here on the floor with you. I want to!!!" "You're the best, Shaun." He turned out the lights and lay down on the floor at the foot of the bed, and I pulled up the covers and went to sleep.

I woke up, and Shaun was still asleep. The voice piped into my head, "You're the king of the Jews," and made me laugh out loud hysterically. This woke up Shaun and freaked him out. He left the room with a strange look on his face. Those fucking operators—what a way to say good-bye to my best friend.

About an hour later, there was a knock at the door. I opened it without asking who it was, and standing there was my sister, Anna. I was really pleased to see her too. She walked in, and I gave her a big hug. The first thing Anna did was order me breakfast. Everyone was feeding me.

There was another knock at the door, and in walked Chandler Newbury, my sister's former fiancé (Willy Wonka, I used to call him), a super nice guy. The three of us chatted, but the conversation was a little awkward. Not like the conversation the night before. The operators started up with their tricks again. The food arrived, and they said, "Death is on the table, kid. The blueberries are poisonous." I wasn't very hungry, so I did not eat.

Then the doctor arrived. This really put me on guard. He had a large scar on his forehead. He listened to my heart and took my blood pressure. Then he pulled out a syringe and proceeded to fill it. You know I hate needles. "What is that?" I asked. "Lorazepam." "I don't want it. I fine without it!" Then Anna said, "When we go to the airport, there will be a lot of people. You should take it." "NO."

Then the operators started. "He's going to kill you with that needle, kid. It's poison. Look at his forehead—he had a device too."

The doctor said, "O K," and left. I remember thinking that was a waste of money.

Anna asked, "Are you ready to go to Memphis?" "If we have to!"

The three of us rode down the elevator and stepped out in front of the hotel. I turned to Chandler and asked sarcastically, "Are you coming with us?" "No, I think I'll sit this one out."

Anna and I stepped into a limo.

CHAPTER 39

The Trip to Baptist Memorial Hospital

Once we were inside the limo headed toward the airport, the operators of the Experiment started. "The limo driver is the Mob, kid, sent by ABS to protect you, and he is Catholic."

We arrived at the airport and got out of the limo, and Anna paid him. Anna and I walked into the airport to the ticket counter. My family had arranged medical emergency tickets for us. The operators would not let me sign my name, so I made a makeshift "F" and drew a line. Then Anna and I walked to the gate.

While we were waiting to board, the black ticket agent came up to us and said, "The signature does not match." Anna said, "It will be OK." I gave the agent an intimidating stare down and started to walk toward him, and Anna restrained me. He took one look at me and left.

We boarded the plane.

We took off, and the operators started up. "Roll like a pilot when hallucinations happen, kid." I began to hallucinate. "Roll right, kid." The hallucinations stopped. They began again. "Roll left." They stopped. This went on for a while.

Then they said, "What gender is Anna?" as they made me hallucinate changes in Anna's face. They altered Anna's face for about twenty minutes.

After this they said, "Kid, you have control of Air Force One in your mind when you're up here. Air Force One just blew up, and it's your fault! Bill Clinton was on the other Air Force One, though. You do know that there are two Air Force Ones, right?"

Then they let me sleep.

I woke up as we touched down in Memphis.

Anna and I deplaned and were met by my mother and father. We all walked to the car.

While we were in the car, my father kept repeating, "That was just perfect!"

We pulled into Baptist Memorial Hospital, and I went on guard. As we got out of the car, I said, "I do not need to go to a hospital right now!!!" My father said, "Oh yes, you DO!!!"

We walked into the waiting room. While we were waiting, Anna and mother invaded my personal space and got really close and hugged me and kept hugging me. They both kept repeating, "Do you feel like we're smothering you?" This was very strange behavior, I thought.

Then a very effeminate male nurse came out to admit me. He took me into a small room and asked me the standard questions, while he flirted with me. He asked what year it was, and the operators told me to tell him the wrong year, so I did. He admitted me to the psychiatric care unit of Baptist Memorial hospital, controlled by the University of Tennessee Medical.

CHAPTER **40**

Baptist Memorial Hospital

I was initially admitted under the care of Dr. Albright.

My family and I were in my room, and I was very tight-lipped, so they said good-bye and left for the day.

I got up and went to go the bathroom in my room, and the door to the bathroom swung freely, and the operators said aloud, "The door swings both ways. If you disclose information to the doctors, things will just get worse!" I went into the bathroom and sat down on the toilet and took a shit and contemplated my fate. I finished in the bathroom and lay down in my bed.

Dr. Albright and all of his interns came into my room. Dr. Albright asked, "So, what happened to you, kid?" I hated that he used the word "kid" to refer to me, and it put me on guard. "Well, I took a trip to Europe and spent a lot of family money. And I'm not bipolar. I have a problem with drugs and alcohol. I have been off of my Lithium for over a month because I believe it does not do anything for me, and I have a hard time tolerating it." Dr. Albright countered, "Well, your parents believe you're bipolar and so does Dr. Underhill." "Who made my parents shrinks, and Dr. Underhill diagnosed me bipolar based on a fifteen-minute conversation and based largely on my parents' input," I replied. "Interesting," Dr. Albright answered. "Would you be willing to go on a drug I prescribe after talking with you further?" "I suppose so." Then the entire entourage left.

Part of the reason I had told Dr. Albright and his interns this was I was trying to recover my flight medical and change my medical status.

I got up from my bed and began my old trick of pacing the halls. I walked the edge of the walls right down to the security doors, crossed, and came back up the edge of the other walls. After my third round, I stopped at the security door and peered out the window. Then a large black nurse came up to me and told me not to cross the line on the floor that led to the security doors and elevator doors and the outside world. So I inquired about his request, pointing at the line on the floor. "You do not want me to cross that line, right?" He responded, "Right." "So, how do I get back to my room, if I cannot cross that line?" "Come on, man," he replied. "Did you or did you not tell me that I could not cross that line?" I questioned, standing on the other side of the line from him. "Yes, but you can cross it once to get on my side of the line." "So the rules are made to be broken even in the psychiatric ward, huh?" "You're pushing it, man. Get on this side of the line." So I crossed line and stayed on the correct side the rest of my stay, but I did pace directly up to and along line the rest of the day.

The next day my family came to visit. My father walked over to the curtains at the window and grabbed the pull rods, one in each hand, and said, "What are these?" While he asked this, the operators of the Experiment filled what I think was the ventricles in my brain and moved them, or something like the ventricles, but they definitely moved something on either side of my brain coordinated with this question. This really pissed me off. So I began to cry and told my mother I had demons in my head that plagued me. Dirty pool begets dirty pool. Obviously my family knew a hell of a lot more than they were telling me. They left for the day.

So I walked out in the hallway, and there was a protective plastic cover over the fire alarm, and I figured it would set off a preliminary alarm, so I removed it. The nurse came running out of nurses' station, looked the opposite direction of me, and then turned and saw me holding the plastic cover. She ran toward me shaking her head and yelling, "No." When she got to me, I calmly asked, "How do I put this back on? SORRY!!!" "Don't fuck with me!!!" I thought to myself.

This was when I concluded that Dr. Paxton and Charter Lakeside Hospital and Dr. Albright and UT Medical and someone from the operators of the Experiment were working together.

Then one of the young interns came in and asked me to re-count my trip to Europe. I began by asking him if he played chess. He responded, "Yes, I enjoy a good game of chess." And we proceeded to play a mental game of chess, and I told him of my travels. I took a liking to this young man.

The next day my family came in "pitching a bitch." "You set off the fire alarm yesterday, and they wanted to send you to Metro. Anna had to talk them out of it!!" my father roared with his almighty finger of authority pointed inches from my nose and with his blood-red face. I thought to myself, "Oh, he thinks he has control in a psycho ward—what a joke!" And calmly I said, "All I did was take the cover off the fire alarm." "Well, it set off an alarm at the nurses' station," my father roared back. They calmed down a bit. Then my father said, "So, you went to St. Andrews. Your mother and I would have liked to have taken a trip like that! Why didn't you stop and see the relatives you drove right by?" I remember thinking, "How did he know my route?" Then I decided to tell him about the rental car. "Oh, I left the Alamo rental car that I rented in Glasgow at Stansted Airport car garage, level two, section B." That shut him up. He did not know what to say. He finally said, "I guess we better make some calls," and all of my family left.

Then Dr. Albright and his whole entourage came in, and he said, "We would like to put you on a drug called Tegretol. We think it will help you a lot more than Lithium did. Would that be OK?" "Sure, I'll give it a go!" And I began a regimen of Tegretol.

A couple of hours later, a young, blond-haired, blue-eyed male intern came in for just a moment and said, "I do not think you have a problem with masturbation," and then he turned around and left. The voice said aloud, "Where did blondie-blond go? He's cute." I got a hard-on, but I was not going to start jacking off at the hospital. I knew this trick. So I got out of bed and paced the halls until my dick went limp.

Once my dick was under control, I went back to my room and never masturbated my entire stay at Baptist.

The next day my family showed up, and my father said, "You know UT Medical offered to pay your travel expenses." "Why would they offer to do that, Dad?" I queried and shrugged my shoulders. He was at a loss for words and did not answer me. We had a little small talk, and my family left after a brief stay.

Then a whole group of interns came into my room, and I was standing at the window looking out at Memphis' Pyramid. I said, "You guys need to let me out of here! I can survive out there on my own. I do not need social programs or UT Medical holding my hand!!!" One of the doctors said to the rest of them, "I find it refreshing."

The next morning they moved me from the lockdown psychiatric ward to a bed in behavioral health. This was a pleasant change. A nicer room, real food, and real silverware. Freedom to move about the hospital. The little things.

I met Dr. Beaconsfield for the first time. He was the "druggy" doctor, king of drug abuse, a former user and one weird motherfucker. All of the interns were standing around him in my room said, "THIS IS THE DOCTOR FOR YOU, BILL."

The next day Dr. Beaconsfield and I had a discussion of all the street drugs I had used and how they had affected me.

The following day we had a meeting with my family and Dr. Beaconsfield and all the interns. Dr. Beaconsfield informed my family that I was not bipolar but was a recovering addict. And as a precaution, they had me on Tegretol, which was used for bipolar and detox. I could see the anger on my father's face as he asked Dr. Beaconsfield, "Does Billy need to go through rehab?" "NO," Dr. Beaconsfield replied with a smile. The meeting ended, and my family left.

Two days later I was discharged from the hospital.

CHAPTER 41

No Future in Memphis

On the ride home from the hospital, the entire family bitched at me, saying, "You really snowed the doctors at the hospital!!!" They treated me like shit that night.

Anna flew home the next day.

Mother bitched at me every day, saying, "You know your father had to borrow money from Max Beathan to pay for your episode and hospitalization." "But didn't UT Medical offer to pay?" I thought to myself.

Then my father informed me I had to get a job, a hopeless endeavor.

First, I tried Roadshow BMW. The industrial psychologist was a real prick and played games with me, and I received no job offer.

Second, Merrill Lynch. I took all the tests and got no job offer.

Third, I tried Prudential. The office manager was a real bitch. She informed me that all my test scores were very low. She told me that I did not have the proper wardrobe. My golf game was not up to par. Finally, that I didn't know anyone in Memphis. How the hell did she know my golf handicap, and I could have taken the series 63 and sold across state lines. Nonetheless, no job offer, what a bitch.

Fourth, I tried Hillard Lyons, a securities firm, and I met with a really nice guy. But the operators sabotaged me on the test, and he thought I was scared of the telephone. I was a phone clerk at the CME, for god's sake. Not his fault. But I did not get a job.

Fifth, James Davis, a clothing store, the brush-off. "I could offer you a position in men's sportswear, but you would not like it."

Sixth, the Zegna store, not even a consideration.

Seventh, the camera store. A flat no. No position available. This was better than bullshit.

Finally, Blockbuster Video, a job. I was given a choice of what store to work at. I chose Chickasaw. I worked two weeks, and they made me manager. I was making $13, 500 as a manager of a small Blockbuster Video. Boring, boring, boring. The operators were constantly piping in homosexual thoughts and accusing me of being a past cocaine and pot dealer.

All of my belongings were in Aspen, and my father refused to pay my back rent to Raymond Marrow or let me go to Aspen to pick up my things. I forfeited everything to Raymond. This was not Raymond Marrow's fault.

My bounced check for three hundred dollars to the Plaza showed up at my parents' address in my forwarded mail, and I paid it and overdraft fees with my Blockbuster money.

My parents were nearly impossible to live with.

Finally, Trent Seaton called me from Chicago and invited me to come live with him. I caught a flight to Wichita picked up my car at Arthur's and drove to Chicago. I had just enough money from Blockbuster to do this. My parents were horrified.

CHAPTER 42

Drifting

I arrived at Trent's place and I was glad to see him. I told him that I would like to try my luck at exchange again. He said, "Give it a few days. You just got here. I'll nose around for jobs for you at the exchange." We met up with Barry and Nathan. I couch surfed a little, happy to be back among friends.

A week after I had arrived in Chicago, Trent informed me that he had arranged a meeting with Greg Ramsey at the exchange. Trent and I got up early Monday morning and drove down to the Merc. We parked in currency's parking across the river from the Merc. Walked across the bridge and entered the Merc. Trent directed me to Greg Ramsey's office. I went in and introduced myself. He was very kind and offered me a yellow jacket for floor access. I noticed on his desk an eight-by-ten glossy picture of him shaking hands with Al Gore. He then said, "I want you just to stand in the S & P aisle near the pit for an hour—can you do that?" "Sure."

I went to compliance, got my yellow jacket, and went and stood in front of his brokers in the S & P pit. The operators of the Experiment rapid-fired the neurons and ran all kinds of images through my head, so I casually stood there for two hours and held a few conversation with people. The Brits had trained me well. This was easy. What were they expecting of me to freak out or something. Greg Ramsey from the other side of the pit came walking over toward me saying, "He's way to use to this!!!" Everyone in the pit nodded in agreement. I guess I passed the test. He walked up to me and said, "I do not like Henry Bandoni." I countered and said, "I like Henry. He gave me my start in this business. He gave me a chance—he believed in me when no one else would."

Then Greg Ramsey offered me an arb clerk position in the S & P pit. On the third day I was late, and the head clerk said as I walked up to the pit, "Oh no, you knew what time we opened." On Friday all the pit clerks bounced me off the steps and out of the pit—I knew then I was done. Then Greg's partner, Andrew Keates, came to the pit on the close and pulled me aside and said, "Bill, I'm going to have to fire you, and I cannot tell you why." He then handed me a sealed envelope. I said, "Thanks for the chance." He walked away. I opened the envelope, and it was an unsigned paycheck. This pissed me off. I was pretty much set up from the start, but this took the cake. So I rode the escalator down and caught them (Greg Ramsey, Andrew Keates, and the rest of their brokerage group) getting on the elevator. I said, "You forgot to sign the check," and handed to Andrew, and he signed it.

I went to the Merc bank and cashed it.

Then I went to Burger King and got some food and sat down

and started eating it. In walked the filling brokers I had worked for that week in the S & P pit and placed an order to go. As they walked out, I waved, and they waved back. What did they think I was going to do? Sign it myself, forging the signature?

The blank check, the cooperation of the operators of the Experiment while I stood in the aisle, the hatred of Henry Bandoni, and the picture of Al Gore—why did I even try??????????

I hung out in Chicago with my friends for a couple of more weeks and had a great time.

Then I headed up to Madison, Wisconsin, and hung out at the Sigma Chi house for a couple of nights.

After that, I aimed the BMW for UNL. I arrived in Lincoln, Nebraska, and went to my favorite watering hole, Cliff's pub. I ran into an old friend, Andy Philcott, unannounced. He agreed to let me live with him for one month for a fee.

First I tried my luck at a securities firm that had an ad in the paper. The guy was a real ass. He used me as a commercial, just like his radio show, and then did not hire me.

Then I stopped by Rothchild's and asked Paul Redmonds if Harry, the general manager of the company, would hire me at Landon's in Omaha. Harry agreed to hire me at the Big and Tall Shop attached to Landon's. I was working with another new kid. I worked two days, and the Landon's salesmen came over while I was making sales and made mocking comments. Everything was a joke to them. Then, on the third day, one of the Landon's salesmen came over and opened the cash register drawer and took money out and left the drawer open and left. I watched the whole thing. Then the kid I was working with saw the open drawer and said, "The drawer is open!" I said, "Really." "I'm going to go tell someone," and he did. Another setup, but what could I do?

Harry called me into his office the next morning. He pulled out a letter opener and proceeded to masturbate with it (or at least run it up and down his crotch) while he fired me. The operators of the Experiment said inside my head while he did this, "Screw the mail, kid." I asked, "Was there money missing?" Harry replied, "Yes, and I've decided to fire both of you." Again, what could I do? Harry was a first-class prick anyway!

I hung out at Andy's and watched *CNN News* and smoked pot with all my college buddies; it was a good time.

After a month, Andy said, "You have to move out, Bill. Ruben Vaughan said you can live with him." The problem was Ruben was a fairly big drug dealer, and I won't live with drug dealers—it's one of my rules! Andy was serious—he dismantled my bed in my room to make the point. So I called Arthur, and he said, "Come back to Wichita."

So I hocked some CDs for gas money and took the short drive to Wichita. I rolled into the Wichita Country Club around dinnertime and went in the men's grill and called Arthur. He said,

"Wow, I did not think you were coming this quickly. No problem—you're always welcome."

I lived with Arthur for two weeks and looked for work. Wichita had nothing to offer.

So I aimed the BMW westward, back to paradise, Aspen.

I arrived in Aspen in the evening and valet-parked my car at the Jerome and went in for a drink. Luckily, I ran into Ashcroft, who offered to put me up a couple of nights. I spent the night at Ashcroft's and in the morning went to the Grand Aspen Hotel. The hotel offered me my PBX job back, and I started the next day.

Ashcroft suggested I move into the hostel at the Little Red School House, so I did.

CHAPTER 43

The Grand Aspen Hotel

Working as a PBX operator was simple for me. I already knew the job. The toughest part was getting up early enough in the morning.

Troy Barrington was now general manager. He had been head of sales when I worked PBX before. Troy was a really nice guy and was very good to me.

I worked the PBX position for about a month and got to know everyone very well. The hotel had a lot of gay employees, and everyone thought I was gay, so I fit in well.

Then Chuck, the reservations manager, was running the operation by himself, and fall reservations were starting to pick up, so he offered me a position in reservations, at the advice of Troy Barrington. By the way, Troy was not gay; he was married with children.

I learned the reservationist position quickly. I could speak very quickly on the phone and typed quickly using my hunt-and-peck-method. I was a star in this position.

After two weeks in this position, the head of maintenance took me over to the Bavarian Inn, a property the hotel group owned for employee housing. He showed me a one-room cabin behind the main building of the Bavarian Inn. I don't remember exactly what the rent was, but it was very reasonable. He offered the place to me and said he could arrange to have the rent taken out of my check pre-tax. I jumped at the chance.

So I moved out of the Little Red School House and into my private cabin. The one-room cabin was pretty cool. It had wood paneling halfway up the walls and a stone fireplace that did not work. A small kitchenette had two gas burners and a small sink with a mini fridge under the burners. The bathroom was a separate room and full size, with a large tub and sink. There was also a small closet. The bed was a double. And there were two small windows with a view of Shadow Mountain. There was a small grass area right out in front of my door, leading up to the main building of the Bavarian Inn.

It was still late summer when I moved in, and the walk to work was about a mile, a perfect walking distance to and from work to get my legs in shape for skiing.

Chuck gave me a small color TV a week after I moved into my cabin, and there was a live cable wire. I was all set.

I became good friends with Adam Smythson, who worked the front desk.

One day Adam and I walked home to the Bavarian Inn

together. He lived in the third and top floor bedroom of the main building of the Bavarian Inn.

We walked into his bedroom. The doorway to the balcony was already open, and I stood next to the doorway. He walked across the room, unbuttoned his black jeans, and ripped off his Grand Aspen Hotel work shirt and kicked of his shoes. He sat down on a shelf across the room. The sunlight was shining down on him. He sat there basking in the sunlight, which hit his long, tan, slightly cut, 'silky smooth' upper torso. His black hair was somewhat ruffled. He was wearing a seashell necklace around his neck. Below his waist, his firm ass and toned legs were encased in his unbuttoned, open fly, 501 black jeans. His large, stiff package was hidden by white Jockey briefs. He had a pearly white smile, and his baby-blue eyes glaring at me were the real killer. Young, pure sex!

The operators of the Experiment piped into my head, "Check him out. He's cute—those baby blues and tall, slender body. He wants you, kid!"

I stood there smiling and flirting for about fifteen minutes. Then I said, "Do you ever pee off this balcony and have sword fights?" I turned and walked out of the room. As I walked down the stairs of the main building of the Bavarian Inn, I thought to myself, "Adam is definitely gay. Do I want him? Have the operators converted me?" I was confused. I walked across the grass to my cabin and went inside.

I lay down on my bed unbuttoned my fly of my black jeans and masturbated to the image of Adam basking in the sunlight.

Was this my image or that of the operators of the Experiment? I was so confused. I blew an oversize load and lay there really bewildered. "Working at the Grand Aspen Hotel was dangerous," I thought to myself, but I seemed happy.

The next day at work I saw Adam. I was friendly but not overly so.

Over the next month, every time I masturbated, the operators of the Experiment piped in the image of Adam basking in the sunlight. After that, they piped in more vivid sexual activity of Adam and me having sex. I saw Adam every day at work, and our friendship was growing. Things were becoming very complicated.

So I invited Adam to dinner; he would not go. I invited him to go to a movie; he would not go. I invited him everywhere, but he would not do anything with me. But he always flirted with me at work. All he wanted was sex, or so it seemed.

So, after a couple months, reservations were slow, and I was hanging out at the front desk, and I asked half-jokingly, "Do you give good HEAD?" He was pushing a bellman's cart across the lobby and turned and said, "YES, are you going to do the same?" All I could do was laugh. Then, from across the lobby with the bellman's cart, he turned and said with a big gay smile, "I guess SO!"

That night there was a knock at the door of my cabin. I got up and answered it. Adam was standing there with a big smile. I invited him in. He sat down on the couch next to me; he extended his right pinky finger. I wasn't really up on fag signals, but I figured this meant he wanted sex. I picked up my stone pipe and loaded it with pot, and we proceeded to get high. On his second drag, he lubed up the end of the pipe with a lot of saliva. I put it in my mouth and thought, "Oh, shit!"

So I asked, "Adam, what religion are you?" "I was baptized Catholic." "Well, then you're Catholic, and so am I." I was really thinking about having sex with him, but I just could not do it. I'm not a homosexual, in spite of all the hard work the operators of the Experiment had put in on me. I just cannot have physical sex with a man. The fantasies coupled with masturbation are one thing. I pretty much have a choice during these fantasies: either blow a load or fight it and be in agony. But the actual sexual contact with a man—so far, I cannot do it! Then I asked Adam, "Are you a FAG?" "You'll have to remind me not to beat you up." He would not come out and admit his sexual preference to me. I thought that was strange. He leaned forward on the couch and extended out his butt as he stood up to leave. As he walked out the door, he said, "You know, Bill, you want to be the dominate one!" and left.

After that, Adam and I were strictly friends. He never made sexual advances toward me again, and I don't think I did either. But whenever I masturbated, the operators had me fantasize about Adam.

The ski season came quickly, and the Grand Aspen Hotel offered me a discounted two-day-a-week pass that came out of my check. I loved to ski Aspen Mountain.

I booked my parents into a suite at the hotel for Christmas week.

Christmas came, and it was good to see my parents. I took them to my cabin, and they made jokes about it. This pissed me off a little. Then my father asked me to go for a drive with him in the rental car. The conversation was going pretty well, until under his breath, he said, "It must have been some soup. What did you do?" And laughed. Oh, I was pissed. He actually knew about sperm soup in Chicago prior to Charter. That the operators had told me was laced with AIDS. I did not say another word the rest of the car ride!!!

I was very distant toward my parents the rest of their stay. I did give my mother a hug upon their departure.

In March I had an appointment with Dr. Laverick for severe headaches, and he arranged a CAT scan in Glenwood Springs, Colorado, with Alexis Wong, MD (Brown and Yale educated) on March 22, 1996, at Valley View Hospital, MRI BRAIN WITH CON 70553, LEVEL C, ID#42700018, ACT#V11849528.

I do not know if these doctors found anything or not, but I was looking for the device. No one admitted knowledge of the Experiment. So, I had had to come up with a new plan.

I decided to go see my cousin's Olivia and Khalil in Paris, France, and see if I could work some magic with a doctor over there.

I called Northwest and booked a month-in-advance ticket to Paris.

Three days prior to my departure, I asked Adam, "Do you want to go with me?" "Go where?" "Paris."

The next day I went into Pitkin County Bank and deposited a fifteen-hundred-dollar rubber check against my First Tennessee account into my Aspen account. The following day, I went back to Pitkin County Bank and asked the receptionist for a pen. She handed me a red ballpoint. I wrote a check for thirteen hundred, and they cashed it. THANK YOU.

I went out to the airport and purchased my ticket in cash from Northwest. Then I went to a local luggage store, the Baggage Claim, and bought luggage for my travels on another hot check.

I went home and did wash and pack my bags. Adam was also doing wash in the basement of the Bavarian Inn, and I ran into him. I was friendly toward him. He had a ball cap on; he kept taking it off and on as he talk to me.

The next morning, I went to Aspen Drug to get my prescription filled. They told me that Rocky Mountain HMO system was down, so they could not fill it. I offered to pay cash. They refused. Disgusted, I left. I went to another pharmacy—same story, so I wrote a check. I asked the cute young female assistant if she wanted to go to Paris with me. She replied, "I'd love to, but I'm taking my state pharmacy boards next week."

I caught a cab to the airport.

CHAPTER **44**

Paris

There was a weather delay out of Aspen to Denver. I spotted an old friend from Wichita, Quincy Dawson, and his boys in the waiting area, but I did not say hello. Finally we boarded for Denver.

Then I caught a flight from Denver to Frankfort. In Frankfort, I sat next to US Air Force boys and eavesdropped on their conversation. Then I boarded the plane.

From Frankfort it was a direct flight to Paris.

I caught a cab to Olivia and Khalil's place. I had gotten the address from Olivia's mother, my aunt Anne Marie, before I left. This was not a manic wild goose chase. The cabbie drove right past the flat. I said, "Where is it?" "DONDE?!!!" He slammed on the brakes and pointed behind us. I got out of the cab and paid him. I saw two friendly-looking guys on the street and said, "Do you speak English?" "A little." I asked them where the address was. They pointed me one block back. I walked up to the door and rang the bell for El-Mazri, but no answer. So I went across the street to a hotel and asked to use the phone. I looked up the number in the book and called Olivia. Olivia answered. "Hi, Olivia, it's Billy Nicholson. I'm across the street can you put me up for a few nights?" "Sure. Ring the bell—'V' for victory."

I walked across the street and Olivia and Jacque, her son, greeted me.

The operators of the Experiment were pretty much lost on this trip. They bounced a little bullshit off me on the way over. But once we were inside the flat, they shut up.

Khalil came home, and they cooked me a fantastic dinner.

Khalil asked, "What would you like to do while you're here?" I would like to see a psychiatrist and take in the sights. Khalil offered to get his convertible Volkswagen bug out of storage for me to drive. I declined and said, "I'll just walk everywhere. You're in the city, and I can take cabs.

They gave me Jacque's room to sleep in. I woke up late and walked out into the living room, and no one was around. But there was a map and money on the floor and a note from Olivia that said, "Enjoy, Billy. We will see you tonight."

I walked along the Seine river and saw the Eiffel Tower and Norte Dame. I had some bread and cheese in a restaurant. Then I walked back to the flat.

That evening they took me out to a restaurant and informed me that I had an appointment with a doctor the next afternoon.

I woke up the next day and Olivia took me by cab to the American Hospital of Paris, and she registered me and paid for everything. Dr. Beaumont came out and said, "Hello, Bill, I understand you want speak with me." "Yes, Dr. Beaumont, I do," I said as I shook his hand. He was an older, kind, gentle man. We went into his office. I started in. "I have been diagnosed paranoid delusional, bipolar, and recovering addict. I am currently on Tegretol." "Do you take any street drugs?" "I smoke a lot of marijuana." "Does anything else trouble you?" "Yes, I also believe I am subject to both biological and psychological experiments by the US federal government. I also believe that in February of 1993 and later the government tried to kill me and blame it on my employer!" Then, under his breath, he whispered, "You're right!"

"Can I make some suggestions?" he asked. I said, "Please." "Stop taking Tegretol and stop smoking marijuana. I want to put you on a common, cheap antipsychotic, Loxapine. Will you take it?" "Yes."

"I want to see you again before you leave, OK?" "OK." He then said, "The woman you're with, your cousin, is a very enchanting woman." "I agree." "Let's go say hello." We walked out, and he introduced himself to Olivia and asked, "Can Bill come see me again before he leaves, and here is a prescription for him." Olivia answered, "Of course he can. Thank you, Dr. Beaumont." We left the hospital.

I hung out with my relatives for another few days, walking around Paris buying posters, and I let one street artist do a sketch of me.

Then we went back to see Dr. Beaumont. He asked, "I know you're here on vacation, but would you like to stay here and pursue your predicament with me?" "I don't know." "Well, if you go back to the United States, you have to trust your doctors and tell them what's going on." I should have stayed, but I was worried about the language barrier and employment. Dr. Beaumont and I shook hands, and we departed as friends. The only man on earth who ever told me truth. His suggestion of an antipsychotic was excellent. It blocks the receptors and inhibits the ability of the operators to control the neurons and brain function. Marijuana also does this by sticking to the receptors, but it does not block them as well and the side effects are counterproductive. The hybrid atypical antipsychotic Zyprexa works the best for me today. It does not stop the control over me, but it does inhibit it. Depakote, which is a crossover drug, originally an anticonvulsive drug, also is a control inhibitor. These give me a slight edge.

When I told Olivia and Khalil about Dr. Beaumont's offer of staying in Paris and remaining under his care, they encouraged me to do so. They told me that Olivia could teach me French, and I could be a waiter.

Then Khalil had a business trip coming up to Madagascar, and he wanted me to go with him. He was a coffee and cocoa broker and trader.

All kinds of good opportunities, and I took none of them. I think the operators were playing dirty pool and influencing me to leave. They would have lost me forever, if I had stayed. What would have happened if I had gone to Madagascar? I might have talked Khalil into taking me to Cairo on the way back. Would they have had control over me in Madagascar or Cairo?

I spent a few more enjoyable days with Olivia, Khalil, and Jacque, and the night before I left, Khalil offered to give me some money. I declined. I flew back to Aspen.

When I arrived in Aspen, it was late afternoon, so I called Dr. Spencer and made an appointment the next afternoon. I went to sleep and woke up late morning. I took a shower and shaved and got really presentable and went in to see Troy Barrington. I told Troy I went to Paris and saw a neurosurgeon, and I might go back. I asked if he wanted me to move out of the cabin. Troy probably would have given me my job back if I asked, but I did not. He said, "OK, Bill, move out of the cabin by the end of the week." "Thanks, Troy."

I went to see Dr. Spencer next. I went into his office and sat down. He said, "Hello, Bill." "Hello, Dr. Spencer. There is something I need to tell you." "What's that, Bill?" "I think I have a voice." He began to laugh. I continued, "I also believe I'm under experimentation by the government." He was rolling, he was laughing so hard. Disgusted, I stood up and left. I walked down the steps from his office and thought to myself, "I have had it with Aspen and this fucking quack!!!!!!!!!!!!!"

I moved that week!!!!

Conclusion

Since I left Aspen, I have lived in various places.

First, I lived in Denver, Colorado, with my aunt and uncle for three months. Then, I spent time in Memphis, Tennessee, with my parents. After that, I moved to Jackson Hole, Wyoming, for a couple of years. Then, I lived in Phoenix, Arizona, for about a year, only to return to Memphis, Tennessee, again. From Memphis, I returned to Jackson Hole, Wyoming, where I lived for ten years. Then, I moved to Aurora, Colorado, a suburb of Denver, for four years. Now, I live in Boulder, Colorado.

The two times I lived in Memphis, I was unemployed except for a brief employment with Budget car rental. While I lived there, I was handed around to various psychiatrists and in and out of various psych wards. I took many psychotropic drugs and was subject to ECT (Electro Convulsive Shock Therapy). Basically, every time I did something wrong in my parents' eyes, they threw me in the cage.

The first time I was in Jackson Hole, I worked at Jackson Hole

Aviation and, later, Alamo car rental. I left to move to Phoenix and take a job in a collection agency, of which my uncle was part owner. This did not work out, so I took a job at Macy's selling men's suits; this job went well. However, my psychiatrist in Phoenix put me in a hospital, and my parents flew in and snatched me back to Memphis. From Memphis, I returned to Jackson Hole after my parents got sick of having me around.

When I returned to Jackson Hole, I worked for Alamo/National and later Hertz. Finally, I took a job with Jackson Hole Community Counseling Center and became a licensed peer specialist in the state of Wyoming for them.

Both times I lived in Jackson Hole I was under the psychiatric care of Dr. Anchorsmith. He was a really nice guy, and his intellectual prowess was second to none. I enjoyed intellectually sparring with him in our weekly therapy sessions, but he never admitted knowledge of the Experiment and even denied it. He would tell me that he had consulted with all of his collogues at conferences and on the phone, and there was no evidence of an experiment. He was also the ultimate in pharmaceutical experimentation. I must have tried thirty different drugs at very high doses, including pills, needles, liquids, and blood testing. Dr. Anchorsmith took all kinds of images of my head and said he did not find any evidence of a device for an experiment. Maybe he did not find anything, or maybe he did.

After Jackson Hole, I moved to Aurora, Colorado, to dry out. The one favor Dr. Anchorsmith did do for me was Marinol, the stepping stone to get off marijuana. I needed to get of street drugs and alcohol and get away from my friends who had substance-abuse problems as well. I successfully got off pot through the use of Marinol and also stopped the Marinol. I was dry. My friends in Jackson were very sympathetic to my need to dry out prior to leaving Jackson, but they were too strong a trigger for me when I was around them. These friends are dear ones and never offered me any drugs or alcohol after I told them I was drying out and never did any substances around me. But I always had the urge to party when I was around them.

In Aurora, I successfully dried out and held various jobs. I have been clean for almost five years now.

The first two jobs I held in Aurora were an exit booth agent for a car rental agency and a car salesman. I did not hold either of them very long, and I was not a very good employee for either of them.

Aurora was not as much fun as Jackson Hole, but it was a nice place to live and was culturally diverse.

Next, I became a professional truck driver for Werner Enterprises, and I held this job for eight months. The first four months I saw the country as an over-the-road driver. Then I had a net operations route at night between Henderson, Colorado (near Aurora), and North Platte, Nebraska, round-trip. I held that position for another four months before I walked off the job. I did an excellent job for Werner, except for quitting without notice.

While I was living in Aurora I was under the psychiatric care of Dr. Rowbottom, another bozo who never admitted knowledge of the Experiment. He did, however, not jockey around with my medication.

Now I live in Boulder, Colorado.

So, what do you think of the manuscript? Truth or insanity? You be the judge. All I can do is live with it! My only defense either way you look at it (truth or insanity) is psychological warfare (which I have learned over the years) and Depakote and Zyprexa (the only drugs that give me some relief by shutting down the receptors in my brain and helping with sleep at night). If you do believe me (truth), please write your congressman or congresswoman, senator, and the president and ask them to give me freedom from the Experiment!!!!

If you believe I am mentally ill, I hope you enjoyed the book!

Thank you.

Francis William Nicholson II

www.ingramcontent.com/pod-product-compliance
Lightning Source LLC
Chambersburg PA
CBHW022019090426
42739CB00006BA/199